Penguin Monarchs

THE HOUSES OF WESSEX AND DENMARK

Athelstan	Tom Holland
Aethelred the Unready	Richard Abels
Cnut	Ryan Lavelle
Edward the Confessor	James Campbell

THE HOUSES OF NORMANDY, BLOIS AND ANJOU

William I	Marc Morris
William II	John Gillingham
Henry I	Edmund King
Stephen	Carl Watkins
Henry II	Richard Barber
Richard I	Thomas Asbridge
John	Nicholas Vincent

THE HOUSE OF PLANTAGENET

Henry III	Stephen Church
Edward I	Andy King
Edward II	Christopher Given-Wilson
Edward III	Jonathan Sumption
Richard II	Laura Ashe

THE HOUSES OF LANCASTER AND YORK

Henry IV	Catherine Nall
Henry V	Anne Curry
Henry VI	James Ross
Edward IV	A. J. Pollard
Edward V	Thomas Penn
Richard III	Rosemary Horrox

THE HOUSE OF TUDOR

Henry VII	Sean Cunningham
Henry VIII	John Guy
Edward VI	Stephen Alford
Mary I	John Edwards
Elizabeth I	Helen Castor

THE HOUSE OF STUART

James I	Thomas Cogswell
Charles I	Mark Kishlansky
[Cromwell	David Horspool]
Charles II	Clare Jackson
James II	David Womersley
William III & Mary II	Jonathan Keates
Anne	Richard Hewlings

THE HOUSE OF HANOVER

George I	Tim Blanning
George II	Norman Davies
George III	Amanda Foreman
George IV	Stella Tillyard
William IV	Roger Knight
Victoria	Jane Ridley

THE HOUSES OF SAXE-COBURG & GOTHA AND WINDSOR

Edward VII	Richard Davenport-Hines
George V	David Cannadine
Edward VIII	Piers Brendon
George VI	Philip Ziegler
Elizabeth II	Douglas Hurd

STEPHEN ALFORD

Edward VI

The Last Boy King

ALLEN LANE
an imprint of
PENGUIN BOOKS

ALLEN LANE

Published by the Penguin Group
Penguin Books Ltd, 80 Strand, London WC2R ORL, England
Penguin Group (USA) Inc., 375 Hudson Street, New York, New York 10014, USA
Penguin Group (Canada), 90 Eglinton Avenue East, Suite 700, Toronto, Ontario,
Canada M4P 2Y3 (a division of Pearson Penguin Canada Inc.)
Penguin Ireland, 25 St Stephen's Green, Dublin 2, Ireland (a division of Penguin Books Ltd)
Penguin Group (Australia), 707 Collins Street, Melbourne, Victoria 3008, Australia
(a division of Pearson Australia Group Pty Ltd)
Penguin Books India Pvt Ltd, 11 Community Centre, Panchsheel Park,
New Delhi – 110 017, India
Penguin Group (NZ), 67 Apollo Drive, Rosedale, Auckland 0632, New Zealand
(a division of Pearson New Zealand Ltd)
Penguin Books (South Africa) (Pty) Ltd, Block D, Rosebank Office Park,
181 Jan Smuts Avenue, Parktown North, Gauteng 2193, South Africa

Penguin Books Ltd, Registered Offices: 80 Strand, London WC2R ORL, England

www.penguin.com

First published 2014
001

Set in 9.5/13.5 pt Sabon LT Std
Typeset by Jouve (UK), Milton Keynes
Printed in Great Britain by Clays Ltd, St Ives plc

ISBN: 978–0–141–97691–4

www.greenpenguin.co.uk

Contents

For Matilda

Prologue

On a winter's day in 1547 a young boy was given the news that his father was dead. This boy was a prince, Edward, Duke of Cornwall, the son and heir of Henry VIII. He was nine years old.

There is a kind of memory that seems to imprint itself so clearly upon the mind that for the rest of our lives we feel we are able always to recover it; it is preserved as it was for ever. Was it like this for Edward? The words were spoken by his uncle Edward Seymour, Earl of Hertford. It was 30 January, a Sunday, and they were at Enfield Manor in Middlesex. With the new king was the younger of his two sisters, thirteen-year-old Princess Elizabeth.

'The Earl of Hertford declared to him and his younger sister Elizabeth the death of their father.' This was the only record Edward made of the interview. His words read like a public notice: just seventeen of them, spare, factual, revealing no emotion, written almost from the outside of a life looking in.[1]

Elizabeth and Hertford would have made their obedience to Edward; very probably they kissed his hand. He was no longer only a brother or a nephew but a king sent by God to rule them. Did Edward and Elizabeth cry? Edward's earliest biographer said that they did, but on no evidence. Perhaps it felt to them like a nursery game, where children imagine for themselves different and altered lives. But Edward and Elizabeth were Henry VIII's children: one day their father would die and their lives would then change for ever; it was a future from which they had no escape.

Probably the interview felt just as unreal for the Earl of Hertford. For a night he had walked the galleries of Whitehall Palace waiting for King Henry to die. A little time later, in the very early hours of Saturday 29 January, he took his horse for the night ride to Hertford Castle. He and Sir Anthony Browne, Henry's Master of the Horse, were there before three o'clock in the morning. The earl had forgotten to leave the key to recover Henry's will with the king's secretary, Sir William Paget, and so hurriedly he wrote instructions for what Paget, his fixer at Whitehall, should do with it.

As yet Henry's death was a secret even to Edward. It was only once Edward had been escorted by Hertford and Browne to Enfield Manor that Hertford broke the news to his nephew. Late at night on 30 January he wrote to the dead king's council in London, revealing through his pen a telling slip of the unconscious. Hertford referred to Henry as the late king 'who we doubt to be in heaven'; he quickly corrected himself to write 'who we doubt *not* to be in heaven'. Henry VIII was gone: thirty-eight years of magisterial and at times unnerving kingly power were over.[2]

For the Earl of Hertford there was a new king to put on the throne and his own pre-eminence in that king's government to secure. Edward had to be taken to London.

Hertford's plan was for his nephew and monarch to be on horseback by eleven o'clock on the morning of 31 January and at the Tower of London by three o'clock that same afternoon.

As Edward and his entourage were setting off from Enfield, the formal proclamation of his accession as king was already being read out in Westminster Hall:

> Edward VI, by the grace of God King of England, France, and Ireland, defender of the faith and of the Church of England and also of Ireland in earth the supreme head, to all our most loving, faithful, and obedient subjects, and to every of them, greeting.
>
> Where it hath pleased Almighty God, on Friday last past in the morning to call unto his infinite mercy the most excellent high and mighty prince, King Henry VIII of most noble and famous memory, our most dear and entirely beloved father, whose soul God pardon; forasmuch as we, being his only son and undoubted heir, now invested and established in the crown imperial of this realm, and other his realms, dominions, and countries, with all regalities, pre-eminences, styles, names, titles, and dignities to the same belonging or in any wise appertaining . . . [3]

Few would have remembered the last time a monarch was proclaimed to his people. That had been in 1509 when a callow and inexperienced king two months away from his eighteenth birthday had been the great hope for change after the tough rule of his father, Henry VII.

So Tudor England once again had a new king who ruled by

blood, by the law of rightful succession and by God's will. Touched by the divine, he was the protector and judge of his people, as well as the Supreme Head on earth of the English Church his father had made out of the convulsions of schism with Rome. And, as no one could have failed to notice, he also just happened to be a boy.

HENRY VII = Elizabeth of York
b. 1457
d. 1509
(1485–1509)

| Arthur, Prince of Wales | Margaret, Queen of Scots | HENRY VIII b. 1491 d. 1547 (1509–47) | Elizabeth Tudor | Mary, Queen of France | Edmund Tudor | Katherine Tudor |

= (1) Catherine of Aragon — MARY I b. 1516 d. 1558 (1553–58)

= (2) Anne Boleyn — ELIZABETH I b. 1533 d. 1603 (1558–1603)

= (3) Jane Seymour — EDWARD VI b. 1537 d. 1553 (1547–53)

= (4) Anne of Cleves

= (5) Catherine Howard

= (6) Catherine Parr

Edward VI

Unless you are a philosopher you cannot be a prince.

Erasmus of Rotterdam,
The Education of a Christian Prince (1516)

Philosophers, when they cease philosophizing and take up action, are dangerous.

Muriel Spark,
The Abbess of Crewe (1974)

I
'A prince born to King Harry the Eight'

The most striking fact about Edward VI is that he was only ever a child. If today this presents us with the challenge of trying to understand a king who died at the age of fifteen years and eight months, for Edward's subjects it was a really serious political matter. A boy could not rule for himself; he had to rely upon advisers who would do the job of governing in his name till at eighteen he reached his majority.

The new king's courtiers and councillors wrestled for the first time in two generations with a very important question. How should they make Edward the king they needed him to be? This was both a problem and an opportunity. Here was a boy ready to be shaped and moulded in a way that was quite different from a king who came to the throne more or less knowing his own mind. Here was a boy, too, in theory entirely at the mercy of powerful advisers. In the past – as recently as seventy years before – royal minorities had gone horribly wrong. But even putting to one side the political disasters of Henry VI and Edward V in the fifteenth century, it was quite possible for a boy king simply to get lost among the big men and the big politics of his reign, to find himself pushed into the background or hidden away at court.

I myself have always found Edward VI a bit of a mystery. The first picture I ever saw of him was in the *Ladybird Book of Kings and Queens*, a wonderful illustration by Frank Hampson, who more famously drew the character of Dan Dare in the boys' magazine *The Eagle*. To me Hampson's other illustrations in *Kings and Queens* spoke for themselves. There was Henry VIII, huge and jolly, standing on the poop of his great battleship *Henri, Grâce à Dieu*. Elizabeth I, dressed to the nines as Gloriana, scowls at the bath being prepared for her. But Frank Hampson's Edward VI is a blank. He looks on as two of his most powerful advisers, his uncle and John Dudley, Earl of Warwick, have a ferocious argument. Hertford angrily thumps the table, while Warwick draws his sword. Edward appears not to see what is going on in front of him. He is merely an observer of the passions of others, inscrutable and passive.

There are other child kings in English history but Edward stands out from them all. Poor Edward V was king for only eleven weeks in 1483 before he went to the Tower of London and was never seen again. The others are Henry III (who came to the throne in 1216), Edward III (1327), Richard II (1377) and Henry VI (1422). All four reached manhood; if they failed as kings they did so later in life. Our Edward is the Peter Pan of English monarchy. King for nearly seven years, he really never grew up.

So here we have the mystery and challenge of a young life we cannot measure against later adulthood. And yet we can still ask questions. Who was this boy king? What was his temperament and personality? What interested him? What did he think and write? How was he trained to rule? Can we ever know? What I hope to show by the end of this short book is that behind Edward's kingly mask we find a fascinating and at times surprising story, of kingship, power, learning, life at court, friendship, ambition, danger, music and fun. Edward's is a very human story, all the more so because he never lived to celebrate his sixteenth birthday.

When he was nine or ten years old Edward began what he called 'A Chronicle' which was both a private record of his life and an account of public events. Early on he wrote it in the third person, a grammatical tense that, when we are used to the conversational directness of modern autobiography, today sounds remote and abstract. In a sense there were two Edwards in the 'Chronicle': the boy who wrote it and the prince and king whose life that boy described.

Edward began his 'Chronicle' with the circumstances of his birth. Here he was precise and factual, recording not only a piece of private history but a decisive event in the life and future of a whole kingdom.

The year of our Lord 1537 was a prince born to King Harry the Eight, by Jane Seymour, then queen; within few days after the birth of her son [she] died, and was buried at the castle of Windsor. This child was christened by the Duke of Norfolk, the Duke of Suffolk, and the Archbishop of Canterbury. Afterward [he] was brought up till he came to six years old among the women.[1]

Edward knew exactly who he was. He knew that his place in the world was settled at birth. He was the son of a king and of that king's late queen. His godfather was the Archbishop of Canterbury, Thomas Cranmer. As an infant he was nursed by women, and when he was six years old he entered the company of men.

Edward was born at Hampton Court Palace on Friday 12 October, the eve of the feast of the translation of Edward the Confessor, the Anglo-Saxon king and saint after whom he was named. He never knew his mother. Queen Jane Seymour died on 24 October of complications from Edward's birth. At eight o'clock on that morning, when the king's physicians reported to Henry that they had more or less given up hope, Jane's spiritual confessor was preparing to give her the last Catholic sacrament of extreme unction.

True to her motto, 'Bound to obey and serve', Jane Seymour, the king's third wife, gave Henry the legitimate male heir he had always wanted. A kind of pro forma circular was sent out in Queen Jane's name on the day of Edward's birth: 'by the inestimable goodness and grace of Almighty God we be delivered and brought in childbed of a prince conceived in most lawful matrimony.' This was all terribly understated. The birth at long last of a prince was interpreted by many as an act of divine providence. Bishop Hugh Latimer of Worcester practically tripped over himself with joy: 'God give us all grace to yield due thanks to our Lord God, God of England; for verily he hath showed himself God of England, or rather an English God.'[2]

On 15 October Edward was baptized by Archbishop Cranmer in the chapel of Hampton Court Palace. It was a grand christening that resonated with meaning, and the most important people in his life played their parts in its ritual choreography. Prince Edward's godmother was his half-sister Princess Mary, the daughter of King Henry VIII and Queen Catherine of Aragon. Mary was twenty-one. Their half-sister Elizabeth, the daughter of the king and Queen Anne Boleyn, was four years old. Elizabeth was carried in the chapel by the eldest of the prince's Seymour uncles, Edward, Viscount Beauchamp, the same man who nine years later as Earl of Hertford was to break to Edward and Elizabeth the news of their father's death. Little Elizabeth carried the holy chrism. Viscount Beauchamp's younger brother, Sir Thomas Seymour, was one of those who held a canopy over his royal nephew. The baby prince was proclaimed Duke of Cornwall.

Edward's birth settled in a moment the royal succession, leaving much less certain the futures of Princess Mary and Princess Elizabeth. To imagine in 1537 that both would one day rule England would have been a staggeringly bizarre notion. Most likely they would be married off to European princes. But here there is a more striking fact. Of the five Tudor monarchs only Edward was ever expected at birth to rule. Henry VII seized the throne by force from Richard III. Henry VIII was king by the death of his elder brother Prince Arthur. Mary became queen because her brother died, and Elizabeth took the crown because Mary died. All but Edward were accidental monarchs. Till the moment he died only Edward was the sole legitimate heir of Henry VIII's body. He was no temporary king: he and only he was England's hope and future.

Edward remembered living 'among the women', and that

is how it must have seemed to a very young boy who in his infancy was cared for by wet-nurses, a dry-nurse, and perhaps four under-nurses, or 'rockers' of his cradle. In charge of them all was an experienced lady mistress, Margaret, Lady Bryan, who had presided over the households of the infant princesses Mary and Elizabeth and probably also the household of Henry VIII's illegitimate son the Duke of Richmond. The names of two of Edward's rockers were Jane Russell and Bridget Forster. His dry-nurse was Sibelle Penne, whose appointment in October 1538 suggests that Edward was being weaned near to his first birthday.

In March 1538 Edward had been given a baby replica of a king's court, with a chamberlain, a vice-chamberlain, a steward, a cofferer and lots of other staff. King Henry and Thomas Cromwell, his pre-eminently powerful minister, chose with great care the men and women to look after the prince. Cromwell interviewed each one of the senior officers. The king appointed as Edward's chamberlain Sir William Sidney and as his steward Sir John Cornwalleys. Sidney was a distinguished courtier in his middle fifties who had commanded a wing of the victorious English army at the bloody battle of Flodden in 1513 and was a veteran too of the king's tiltyard. Cornwalleys had earned his knighthood on a military expedition to France in 1521. Henry VIII valued and rewarded martial toughness and feats of chivalry. These were the kind of men who could protect and raise a young prince in his father's image.

Special instructions drawn up for the prince's officials made plain the great weight of responsibility that rested upon their shoulders. God had given Edward to England for the 'consolation and comfort' of the whole realm. It fell to Sir William 'to have the keeping, oversight, care and cure of his majesty's and the whole realm's most precious jewel the prince's grace' and to foresee 'all dangers and adversaries of malicious persons and casual harms' to Edward.

No chances could ever be taken with Edward's well-being: it was essential to keep him safe and well. Here the rules governing his household were unambiguous. Strangers were forbidden to enter Edward's room. Access to him was permitted on the basis of social rank and it was almost certainly licensed by the king through Cromwell. No one under the degree of a knight could be admitted to the prince's presence, and a visitor would expect only to kiss his hand. New clothes for the prince were thoroughly washed. Edward's servants were forbidden to visit London, a city where plague and infection routinely killed thousands. Kept at a safe distance were the 'poor, the needy and sick resorting to his grace's gate for alms'. Edward's food and drink were closely supervised.[3]

Every so often we catch glimpses of the infant prince. Near the end of 1538 Lady Bryan reported to Cromwell that Edward was 'in good health and merry'. He had four teeth, 'three full out, and the fourth appeareth'. The prince's best coat was of 'tinsel' (material woven through with gold and silver thread) but Lady Bryan fretted that he had no very fine jewel for his cap. She well understood the king's expectations: 'I shall order all things for my lord's house the best I can so as I trust the king's grace shall be content with all.' In March 1539 Lady Bryan wished that Henry and Cromwell had seen Edward dancing and playing to his minstrels 'so wantonly' that he could not stand still. From these very few fragments the prince seems to have been a happy, lively and healthy toddler.[4]

The baby prince received important visitors. In September 1538 Lord Chancellor Thomas Audley thanked Cromwell for the king's licence to visit Edward. 'And I assure your lordship', Audley wrote, 'I never saw so goodly a child of his age, so merry, so pleasant, so good and loving countenance, and so earnest an eye, as it were a sage judgment towards every person that repaireth to his grace.' Praise indeed; but of course Audley knew that to praise the prince was also to praise his father the king.[5]

King Henry's palaces were modified to accommodate the prince's household. A new set of lodgings was built at Hampton Court, complete with presence and watching chambers, a garderobe and bathroom and a privy kitchen. At Greenwich Palace Edward's rooms were next to Henry's. But, following the custom for princes and princesses, for most of the time Edward lived apart from his father. As we will see, to visit Henry VIII was a special treat Edward came to love.

Like any prince, his life was one of removes and travel, settling for a time in various houses a day's ride from London. Some houses were good for the cold winter months, others for summer. Lodgings were built for Edward at three royal houses, Enfield, Tyttenhanger and Hatfield. When Sir William Sidney wrote to Cromwell on 30 September 1538 the household was at Havering in Essex, a few miles to the north-east of London, from where Lady Bryan's letter of 1538 was sent also. Lord Chancellor Audley wrote to Cromwell:

I was right glad to understand there that the king's majesty will have his grace removed from Havering now against winter time, for surely it seemeth to me that the house will be a cold house for winter, but for summer it is a good and goodly air.

By March 1539 Lady Bryan and her charge were at the house and manor of Hunsdon in Hertfordshire, a residence built solidly in fifteenth-century brick but much expanded by Henry VIII, and one of the most familiar to Edward as he grew up.[6]

Edward's portrait was painted late in 1538 by Hans Holbein the Younger, who presented it to Henry VIII as a New Year's gift in January 1539. Henry gave Holbein in thanks a gold cup. This masterpiece of a portrait tells us so much about the very little boy Henry VIII called his precious jewel.

We are lucky enough to be able to compare the picture with Holbein's preparatory drawing of Edward's face. This comparison is a measure of the brilliance of Holbein's final achievement. Where the drawing is delicate and very simple, the painting is by contrast an explosion of intense colours, striking crimson and rich cloth of gold. It commands our attention. Here is a king's son, fabulously dressed, wearing a bonnet and a cap decorated with a white ostrich feather. Lady Bryan's worries about the prince's wardrobe seem far away from Holbein's New Year's gift.

Prince Edward at fourteen months looks straight at the artist with blue-grey eyes. From underneath the bonnet his fine blond hair is combed down straight onto his forehead. The fingers of his right hand are spread apart, his palm open:

here Edward almost touches the viewer. In his left hand he grasps a rattle, holding it as a king does a sceptre. To Edward's whole attitude there is a kind of quietness, a sense of peace, even a gentleness, as well as a feeling of suppressed activity.

In 1536 or 1537 Holbein had painted Edward's mother, Jane Seymour. The finer details of Edward's features are his mother's: the chin with a small point, the delicate lips slightly pursed. But where Queen Jane turns away modestly from the viewer, Edward looks us straight in the eye; and where Jane is passive, Edward challenges. The directness and engagement of Edward's face are notably missing from Queen Jane's. Though Edward's portrait has to it a lightness of touch, even a cheerful playfulness, it has also the easy and confident authority that comes with rank and position. And all this in the picture of an infant.[7]

Holbein's skill as an artist of genius was to make a highly stylized image look natural and instinctive. He knew, after all, what his patron wanted. To paint the heir to the throne was a very serious undertaking for any artist at a king's court. And so Holbein left nothing in the picture to chance or misinterpretation, which is why Edward's portrait has framed within it a Latin text specially composed by the courtier and diplomat Sir Richard Morison. Sir Richard wrote:

Little one, emulate your father and be the heir of his virtue; the world contains nothing greater. Heaven and earth could scarcely produce a son whose glory would surpass that of such a father. Only equal the deeds of your parent and men can wish for no more. Surpass him and you have surpassed all the kings the world ever revered and none will surpass you.

Holbein and Morison were together praising the kingship of Henry VIII as much as they were celebrating Henry's legacy and posterity: they were thinking about both present and future. In 1538 Henry VIII was at the height of his political power, confidently imperial in his kingship. He had at his side the formidable Thomas Cromwell. In breaking with the Church of Rome he believed he had shown the pope who was master. So it was no wonder that Holbein painted a prince who was at a little over one year old very much his father's son: solid, robust, royal and already magisterially in control. And Morison's inscription makes this point forcefully. Here was high praise for a prince, but even more lavish flattery of the king.

A contemporary poet (it may have been John Leland) knew exactly what the effect of Holbein's portrait of Edward was meant to be. He saw it as we are meant to see it. Addressing the infant prince he wrote:

> As often as I direct my gaze to look at your delightful face
> and appearance,
>> So I seem to see the form of
> Your magnanimous father shining forth in your face.
>> The immortal Holbein painted this pleasing picture with
> rare dexterity of hand.

Never had the needs of politics and dynasty more shaped the image of a young English prince, and never were the expectations for that very small boy more obviously and powerfully elevated.[8]

2
'He was brought up in learning'

In July 1544 the household that had cared for Prince Edward since 1538 was broken up on the orders of his father the king. Henry VIII was off to war, the favourite pastime of any great Renaissance prince. While he was away on campaign in France Queen Katherine Parr, Henry's sixth and last consort, exercised the powers of a regent. Edward was now six years and eight months old, no longer an infant, and it was time for him to enter the world of men. Sir William Sidney, who had been Edward's chamberlain for nearly six years, became the prince's steward. Lord Chancellor Wriothesley and Edward's uncle the Earl of Hertford dissolved the old household and the prince's nurses and domestic staff were comfortably pensioned off.

Edward's education began now in a serious and formal way. He described it in his 'Chronicle': 'At the sixth year of his age he was brought up in learning by Master Doctor Cox, . . . and John Cheke, Master of Arts, two well-learned men, who sought to bring him up in learning of tongues [languages], of the scripture, of philosophy, and all liberal sciences.'[1]

Richard Cox was the older man of the two, in his middle forties, a former scholar and fellow of King's College,

Cambridge, a teacher in Oxford and for a number of years the headmaster of Eton College. He was a man to admire but hardly one obviously to like: a clever and reforming headmaster at Eton, he was also a severe disciplinarian. This was a time when one of the secretaries to Edward as king could say that the 'rod only was the sword that must keep the school in obedience and the scholar in good order'. These were words that Richard Cox lived and taught by.[2]

John Cheke celebrated his thirtieth birthday three weeks before the king appointed him to Edward's household. Strictly he was the junior master whose task it was to 'supplement' Dr Cox's teaching 'both for the better instruction of the prince, and the diligent teaching of such children as be appointed to attend upon him'. But Cheke was no simple assistant. He was perhaps the most brilliant classical scholar in England. A student and then a fellow of St John's College, Cambridge, in 1540 he was appointed the king's (or regius) professor of Greek in the university. Cheke lectured on the literature of Homer, Herodotus, Sophocles and Euripides, introducing to Cambridge a revolutionary pronunciation of ancient Greek that supposedly recovered how the language had really been spoken. Cheke irritated the Cambridge old guard and inspired its young men in roughly equal measure. He was a passionate teacher whose pupils adored him. One of those former students, Roger Ascham, wrote in a book he presented to Prince Edward in 1545 how fortunate it was for 'the commodity and wealth' of the whole kingdom that Cheke was now Edward's tutor.[3]

Prince Edward was set to work on the basics of Latin grammar. It was not unusual for young boys of his age to be taught Latin this early in their lives and at first he had much the same kind of education that other boys received in schools across England. The textbook he used was the standard Latin grammar by William Lily, a book later read by Elizabethan schoolboys like William Shakespeare. One of Edward's copies of Lily has survived, printed on vellum and bound in crimson silk. More for display in the library than for the classroom, this copy is illuminated with the feathers and the motto of the Prince of Wales, 'HIC DEN' for 'Ich dien', German for 'I serve'.[4]

In early December 1544 Dr Cox reported to the king's secretary, Sir William Paget, that 'my lord and dear scholar' was making excellent progress in mastering the parts of grammar set out by William Lily. Edward was also learning to obey his masters. Running through Cox's letter to Paget is the tiresome metaphor of military campaign. Just as his father had defeated the French, Cox wrote, so Edward had 'beaten down and conquered' grammar. Cox's preference was always for conquest over encouragement; not for nothing was it once said of him that 'the best schoolmaster of our time was the greatest beater,' words meant by the man who spoke them – the equally ferocious but brilliant Latinist Walter Haddon, who was once Cox's pupil at Eton – as a compliment.[5]

Cox sought with his pupils to break 'an ungracious fellow' he called Captain Will. He broke down any resistance to learning; it was a matter of pride. As he punned grimly to Paget: 'and at Will I went and gave him such a wound that he wist not what to do.' Probably Cox had not actually beaten Edward physically, but he had shown the young prince who was master in the schoolroom. Obedience was the foundation for a strict morality. Cox was explicit here: under his tutelage Edward learned 'how good it is to give ear unto discipline, to fear God, to keep God's command-ment to beware of strange and wanton women, to be obedient to father and mother, to be thankful to them that telleth him of his faults.' This was exactly the thought in Edward's mind eighteen months later when he wrote to Cox: 'I thank you also for telling me of my fault; for they are my friends who point out to me my errors.' In 1546 he quoted to Cox two words from the Latin poet Dio-nysius Cato: '*magistrum metue*' – 'Fear [or respect] your teacher'.[6]

John Cheke was a gentler and more encouraging tutor than Cox, and it is difficult to imagine him carrying the birch brandished by schoolmasters and university teachers in every Tudor woodcut of a classroom scene. He was a bright spark of a man who was not afraid to challenge the old establishment, and who had creative and stimulating ideas about language and literature. Of fairly humble birth, Cheke had succeeded by his scholarly brilliance and by his skill as a courtier. His teaching reflected what his devoted pupil Roger Ascham wrote in *The Scholemaster*: 'young children were sooner allured by love than driven by beating to attain good learning.' Here was an idea that to an accom-plished veteran of schoolroom beatings like Richard Cox would have been bizarre and even dangerous: at school children learned to obey without question. Yet Prince Edward was different to thousands of young boys of his age being drilled by their schoolmasters in Latin grammar. He was taught to be obedient to his masters – but he was being trained to rule too.[7]

Every day at Mass Edward read from the Old Testament some of King Solomon's Proverbs, 'wherein he delighteth much and learneth there how good it is to give ear unto discipline'. Once he had mastered the foundations of grammar he read the famous Latin fables of Aesop and began early in 1545 to learn the 'distichs' of Dionysius Cato. These simple couplets were compact pieces of morality that helped Edward with his Latin. Edward quoted one of them to Richard Cox in a letter of 1546: 'When a poor friend gives you a little present, /accept it kindly, and remember to praise it amply.'[8]

Also in 1545 Edward began to write letters that he copied in his very best handwriting into a copybook. Formal, stuffy and stodgy, they are really exercises in grammar and formal composition. But still they are very interesting, and help us to hear one register of Edward's voice: respectful, formal, correct and eager to compliment. Edward wrote to the most important people in his life, to his father, to Queen Katherine, to his sisters Mary and Elizabeth, to his godfather Archbishop Cranmer of Canterbury and sometimes to Richard Cox. Edward applied himself to the standards and expectations of his teachers and his family. True, his letters were not masterpieces of self-expression, but he was after all only seven or eight years old. They were instead careful exercises in inculcating and embedding very deeply the values of a culture, and they helped to form him as a person.

The young prince quickly learned how to be royal. He

showed respect and deference for his elders. Above and beyond anyone else was Henry VIII, whom he addressed with immense formality: 'O king most illustrious and most noble father!' Always there was a sense of obligation and duty, of the place he knew he occupied as Henry's heir and successor. One of the most telling lines he ever wrote in English was to Queen Katherine: 'I pray God I may be able in part to satisfy the good expectation of the king's majesty my father and of your grace.' These were the heartfelt words of a young boy who perceived already the weight of duty pressing hard upon him.[9]

Edward was introduced to the tricks and vanities of the Renaissance scholar, mocking his own Latin while praising the literary perfections of others. Encouraged by John Cheke he looked for the flourishes of learning. When he received a letter from Queen Katherine which she had written in the elegant roman hand of an accomplished scholar, Edward replied to her with a little story. Cheke, he said, had believed that Queen Katherine's secretary must have written it for her. But then Cheke had looked at her signature and recognized that the letter was perhaps indeed Katherine's work. Seven-year-old Edward was likewise 'much surprised', praising Katherine for her progress in Latin and good literature, 'Wherefore I feel no little joy, for letters are lasting; but other things that seem so perish' – words which, if we take them out of the context of early formal composition done under the supervision of his teacher, make him sound precocious and priggish.[10]

Virtue was a watchword of Edward's letters. Here his tutors stuck fast to values of duty and service that had deep roots in the ancient world, mediated in the early decades of the sixteenth century through the hugely influential scholarship of Erasmus of Rotterdam, who believed that the best kind of prince was virtuous and educated, an enlightened ruler of his people guided by God. And so Edward was raised to believe in the value of knowledge and, for all the wealth and majesty of his father's monarchy, to prefer wisdom to possessions. Letters were better than treasures, he told Richard Cox. He thought of Cicero, who had said the wise man alone was rich. This was in April 1546, when Edward was half a year away from his ninth birthday. Already he was trying to find his own voice and pen. Another letter he asked Cox to accept as his own composition, the fruit of a prince's judgement and labour.

At some point in the spring and early summer of 1546 Edward's portrait was painted. Probably the artist (who may have been Guillim Scrots) did his preliminary work at Hunsdon, for the house can be seen in the picture.

The beautifully dressed and quietly magisterial fourteen-month-old of Holbein's New Year's gift to Henry VIII was by now a maturing boy quite as impressive. In the picture Edward is dressed in a superb gown of russet-coloured satin lined with lynx fur and a white satin doublet embroidered with gold. Where the infant held a rattle in his left hand, the boy holds in his right a long dagger. His attitude deliberately evokes the pose of Henry VIII in Holbein's great mural (since destroyed) of the king and his family that dominated Henry's presence chamber in Whitehall Palace. This was an image of his father, huge and terrifying, that

PARVVLE PATRISSA, PATRIÆ VIRTVTIS ET HÆRES
ESTO, NIHIL MAIVS MAXIMVS ORBIS HABET.
GNATVM VIX POSSVNT COELVM ET NATVRA DEDISSE,
HVIVS QVEM PATRIS, VICTVS HONORET HONOS.
ÆQVATO TANTVM, TANTI TV FACTA PARENTIS,
VOTA HOMINVM, VIX QVO PROGREDIANTVR, HABENT
VINCITO, VICISTI, QVOT REGES PRISCVS ADORAT
ORBIS, NEC TE QVI VINCERE POSSIT, ERIT.

1. 'Little one, emulate your father and be the heir of his virtue; the world contains nothing greater': Prince Edward by Hans Holbein the Younger, 1538

2. Edward's uncle, Thomas, Baron Seymour of Sudeley, who used the king to make a grab for power and was executed for it in 1549

3. Queen Jane Seymour, Henry VIII's third wife and Edward's mother, painted by Hans Holbein the Younger in 1536 or 1537

4. Prince Edward in 1546, with one of his residences, Hunsdon, shown in the far background

5. 'Edward VI, by the grace of God King of England, France, and Ireland, defender of the faith': the young king's coronation medal, 1547

6. 'Young children were sooner allured by love than driven by beating to attain good learning': John Cheke, Edward's tutor as prince and king, in a portrait attributed to Claude Corneille de Lyon

7. A king in profile: Edward, holding the red rose of the royal house of Lancaster, in a portrait attributed to the court artist Guillim Scrots

8. Edward in 1551 by Guillim Scrots: a king of European stature

9. Edward VI and the Pope: an allegory of the triumph of
Protestantism over the false power claimed by the Pope. From his
deathbed Henry VIII points to Edward as his successor. Standing on
Edward's left is his Governor and Protector, the Duke of Somerset.
Sitting next to Somerset are his brother Thomas Seymour and
Archbishop Thomas Cranmer of Canterbury, Edward's godfather.

10. A king looks passively on: Edward VI, Protector Somerset (wearing a gold chain) and the Earl of Warwick by Frank Hampson in the *Ladybird Book of Kings and Queens*, 1967

Edward would have known very well indeed. So the message of the Hunsdon portrait was that here is a prince and a king-in-waiting who would one day take up his father's great dynastic legacy.

We need to look beyond the picture, to be alert to just how much it tells us about the child behind the image. Edward looks straight at the artist. The boy of eight years has very fair skin, cropped auburn hair and clear grey eyes. He gives little away of his feelings. He appears calm and steady. He is not yet commanding, but there is just the whisper of a set jaw that pushes out his cheeks and forms a line of resolution between his chin and lower lip. In other words, in dress and in attitude he is princelike. And that, of course, was the object of the picture – to capture the authority given to him by his birth and the power of his future kingship. Of the boy we have some first impressions: quietly purposeful, sensitive and alert; developing physically; as yet not wholly comfortable with what was expected of him; a child getting used to the idea of what it was to be a king.

Edward looked always to his father, for his blessing and for his love. In early July 1546 he thanked Henry for sending him a skilled musician, Philip van Wilder, who was helping to improve his playing on the lute. He was even happier to be told that he was to visit the king. The stay at Whitehall Palace was short but he was thrilled by it. Henry loaded his son with gifts of valuable chains, rings, jewelled buttons and necklaces. Afterwards Edward wrote to Queen Katherine with 'uncommon thanks, that you behaved to me so kindly'.[11]

Edward now found himself balanced between the private

world of his household and the demands of public duty and display. He knew in early August about the diplomatic visit to Henry's court soon to be made by the Admiral of France, Claude d'Annebaut. Edward was going to help to receive the admiral's embassy. He was a little nervous, asking Queen Katherine by letter whether d'Annebaut knew Latin very well. If he did, Edward wrote, 'I want to learn more what I should say to him when I come to meet with him'.[12]

The admiral's embassy was a tremendous success. Edward saw with his own eyes the splendours of his father's kingly style. On 20 August, to the 'terrible' sound of cannon fired along the waterfront at Bankside and from the Tower of London, d'Annebaut rode 'in great triumph' through the city. Edward met the admiral to escort him to Hampton Court. With the prince were the Archbishop of York, Edward's uncle the Earl of Hertford, the Earl of Huntingdon and 2,000 horsemen. Edward and d'Annebaut embraced 'in such lowly and honourable manner that all the beholders greatly rejoiced'. Taking the place of honour, Edward rode with the admiral to the outer gate of the palace where they were met by the lord chancellor and the King's Council.[13]

The excitements of August began to fade in the first week of September, when once again Edward was claimed by Cheke and the schoolroom. He dutifully wrote out his exercises, framing a letter to his father to thank Henry for his care and for the gift of a buck, hoping to see him again soon. A few weeks later he thanked Queen Katherine for the kindnesses she had shown to him, 'so many ... that I can scarcely grasp them with my mind'. As well as the practice these letters gave him in his Latin, Edward was genuinely thrilled by his first experience of what it was to perform on the public stage of royal theatre.[14]

Any direct conversation between Edward and the Admiral of France had been in fairly limited Latin or through a translator. But any future king of England needed to be able to speak fluent French. Historically France was England's enemy and rival, but also potentially its ally. It is telling that Henry VIII had long wanted to emulate the royal fashions of the French court but also tried as often as he could to go on military campaign against France. Two months after his meeting with Claude d'Annebaut Edward began to learn French with Jean Belmaine, a Protestant refugee who had taught the language to Princess Elizabeth. Belmaine gave Edward his first lesson on 12 October, Edward's ninth birthday. In December Edward wrote in French to Elizabeth to thank her for her last letter, her encouragement and her example.

So here was a prince who was learning quickly and writing with fluency to his family. He knew his obligations. In January 1547 Queen Katherine sent him a New Year's gift of a double portrait of his royal parents – better to gaze upon, he wrote to her in thanks, than any magnificent gift. He wrote very fondly on the same day to his sister Princess Mary. From Hertford Castle in late January he thanked Bishop George Day of Chichester, John Cheke's old teacher at Cambridge, for his present of some volumes of Cicero, 'the prince of eloquence'. He also sent a letter to Archbishop Cranmer, 'most loving godfather, more dear to me than my eyes', on the theme of literature and the liberal arts. He complimented Cranmer on his fine Latin style.[15]

In July and August 1546 Edward had been with his father and stepmother at Whitehall. He had played his part in the embassy of the Admiral of France. He had then gone back to the hard work of the schoolroom with Cheke and Cox, mainly at Hatfield. He played the lute with Philip van Wilder, talked, read the Latin poet Horace, played and received gifts. In letters he reflected upon love, virtue and duty, learning the ways of royal discourse. He signed those letters with affection. To his sister Princess Mary he was 'Amantissimus tui Frater', 'Your most loving brother'. He was a nine-year-old prince growing and learning all the time, by the measure of his own age a whole lifetime away from adulthood.[16]

Edward was at Hertford Castle when he wrote to Archbishop Cranmer on Monday 24 January 1547. Four days later Henry VIII was dead and the prince was now a king.

Hurried back on 31 January to London, Edward VI, 'by the grace of God King of England, France, and Ireland', stayed with his court in the royal lodgings of the Tower of London. Touched by God, there was no other authority in the land. But he could not rule for himself, and the power to govern had to be exercised for him.[17]

At the Tower on the 31st the council of thirteen executor-advisers appointed by Henry VIII met together 'reverently and diligently' to affirm their loyalty to Henry's last will and testament. Meeting together, they decided that they needed a leader, 'some special man' of their number to articulate their corporate will. With the influential Sir William Paget working as the Earl of Hertford's campaign manager, their choice of Hertford was not a very surprising one.

The councillors agreed that Hertford would have 'the first and chief place amongst us' with the two offices and titles of Protector of the king's realms and dominions and Governor of his most royal person. All thirteen executors then signed the statement in the council's new book of its proceedings. First of all the signatures, standing out boldly, was the name 'E. Hertford'.[18]

The following day all the councillors met again in the Tower to hear Henry's will read out from beginning to end, after which they took their oaths to the king. They went to Edward in his private chambers to ask for his consent to their election of Hertford as Protector and Governor. At nine years old Edward had before him his father's executors, the assistant councillors named in Henry's will, and the members of the nobility who were with him at the Tower. All of them kissed his hand. For a boy who was still so new to the theatre of monarchy it must have been overwhelming.

Today we surely find it sad, and perhaps even positively cruel, that a boy so very young was expected to show almost no emotion. Even for a child king grief was always something to be properly disciplined. Words, too, were chosen very carefully. Edward wrote to Queen Katherine and to his sisters Mary and Elizabeth. Thinking of his father in heaven, he assured Katherine of God's rewards for the noble and virtuous. To Mary he emphasized the wisdom of accepting God's will and promised to be her dearest brother. He knew from a letter already sent by Elizabeth that she, like him, was gaining a victory over nature in moderating her grief at their father's death.

Edward was a boy transformed: a child who was now a king, the father of his people. The council planned down to the last word and gesture the form of Edward's coronation in Westminster Abbey. Here Edward VI would be bound publicly to God and to his subjects. This was the duty for which he had been trained: he was both a ruler and a servant who would be held to account by God. Archbishop Cranmer would show the king to his people, declaring: 'Sirs, here I present King Edward, rightful and undoubted inheritor by the laws of God and man to the royal dignity and crown imperial of this realm.' Edward would make his coronation oath and, symbolic of the mystical otherness of being a king, be anointed with holy oils on his shoulders, on both of his arms, on the palms of his hands and on his head.[19]

On 14 February Princess Elizabeth replied to her brother's letter. She made clear her loyalty: 'May God long keep your majesty safe and further advance ... your growing virtues to the utmost.' She addressed Edward as perhaps she had done on the day they heard together the news of their father's death. He was a boy still growing and to his sisters he was a little brother: but above all Edward was now *Rex Serenissime et Illustrissime*, 'most serene and illustrious king'.[20]

3
'To bear rule, as other kings do'

However bright he was, Edward still had a very long way to go before he could rule for himself. At first he was much too young to understand the sometimes tough world of Tudor court politics. He was a boy king who flourished in a lively royal court but whose vulnerability was thrown into sharp silhouette by the ambitions of one of his uncles, Thomas Seymour. Edward VI's growing-up was punctuated by some uncomfortable episodes.

From the beginning of Edward's reign, government was in the hands of Edward Seymour, who by March 1547 had a whole portfolio of impressive titles and offices: Duke of Somerset, Earl of Hertford, Viscount Beauchamp, Lord Seymour, Governor of the king, Protector of his people, realms and dominions, Lieutenant General of his majesty's land and sea armies, Treasurer and High Marshal of England, Knight of the Garter. At first bound to act only with the advice and consent of Henry VIII's executors, very quickly he was free to govern pretty much at will.

Edward was not a kind of half-forgotten prince pushed to one side by his uncle, spending his days only in dreary Latin grammar exercises. True, if anyone wanted to get something done in government or fancied a piece of royal patronage they would speak to Somerset through his officials. Protector Somerset got on with the business of running the country, as he was supposed to do, leaving his nephew free to live as a young king in a busy and lively court. There was every reason to believe that one day Edward would be old enough to rule for himself.

Royal life worked to familiar routines. Edward lived much as his father had done. He was dressed by servants, his meals were brought up to his private chambers from the privy kitchens below stairs. He said his prayers and listened attentively to sermons. He studied his lessons with John Cheke, played and listened to music and saw plays, interludes and masques, in which occasionally he acted. He enjoyed the companionship and conversation of trusted servants. Every few months the court would 'remove' to one of the royal palaces – Oatlands, Richmond and Hampton Court in Surrey, Greenwich in Kent, Windsor Castle in Berkshire and Whitehall and St James's in Westminster. Doubtless Edward had his favourite palaces, but each one had its own peculiar nooks and corners.

Dozens of men and boys were employed to keep Edward busy and entertained. By 1552 forty-two musicians, two singers, six singing children and nine minstrels were on the payroll of the King's Chamber. There were also trumpeters, a harpist, violinists, a bagpiper, a flautist, a drummer and players of the lute, the rebeck, the sackbut and the virginal. Edward played the lute, his proficiency brought on from 1546 by Philip van Wilder, who also directed the singing children of the Privy Chamber. The names of the musicians suggest a lively and international group: there was the

Welsh minstrel Robert Reynolds, from the Low Countries the viol player Hans Horsnett and Peter van Wilder (we can guess that he was Philip's brother), and the Italian violinists Albert de Venice, Ambrosio de Lapi de Milan, Vincent de Venice and Francis de Venice.

Every so often we come across telling snapshots of Edward's life at court. In February 1548, for example, he acted in a Shrovetide masque. Sir Michael Stanhope, the chief gentleman of Edward's Privy Chamber, gave the order for 'garments to be made for six masquers, whereof the king's majesty shall be one, and the residue of his stature, and six other garments of like bigness for torchbearers'. In other words, the twelve masquers were Edward and his young companions.[1]

Hunting was the greatest sporting pursuit of any royal court. Whole departments of men looked after the king's buckhounds and hawks and falcons. There was a keeper of the king's bears as well as a keeper of his mastiffs. Dozens of armourers, bowyers and fletchers made and maintained the weapons and equipment for hunting and for tournaments of chivalry. Edward soaked up all the energy of the tournament and he had a boy's fascination for war, more so as the son of a king who had gloried in combat and loved military campaigning. As early as 1545 Roger Ascham presented to Edward a book he had written on the subject of archery. The young king became highly proficient with a bow.

So we have to imagine a bustling court. The gentlemen of his Privy Chamber, his tutors, visiting courtiers, busy servants, entertainers and musicians, physicians and apothecaries, and young noble companions: Edward was hardly left idle. One of the grooms of his Privy Chamber, John Fowler, wrote in 1548 that Edward was never alone for more than a quarter of an hour. The king's life was packed with activity and people.

Edward had a number of companions at court, young noblemen and the heirs to great titles and estates. Four boys were especially close to the king: Henry, Duke of Suffolk and his younger brother Lord Charles; Thomas Butler, Earl of Ormond; and Ormond's cousin Barnaby Fitzpatrick, the son of an Irish baron. Lord Charles was much the same age as Edward, Duke Henry and Barnaby two years older.

To these boys Edward was both a friend and a king who gave commands, a fact that made his letters to Barnaby, who by 1552 was away on an embassy to Paris, a peculiar mix of friendly candour, gossip, high moral tone and kingly bossiness. Edward certainly knew who was in charge.

His young friends were boys of talent and promise. Barnaby Fitzpatrick was taken under the wing of some of Edward's most experienced officials. Duke Henry and Lord Charles were universally praised (indeed probably over-praised) for their achievements, their reputations for brilliance enhanced by their untimely deaths in an outbreak of sweating sickness in Cambridge in 1551. Here Edward is frankly a mystery: in his 'Chronicle' he made not one reference to the deaths of these two young men, lauded for their virtues and talents by John Cheke and his scholarly circle. Perhaps they were too painful for him to record. But other celebrations of the boys' lives give us some impression of the companions they were for Edward. Henry waited on the king in his private chambers, and one writer, Thomas Wilson, who was close to Cheke, wrote in praise of the young duke 'that few were like unto him in all the court'. Lord Charles was a gifted scholar and a talented musician and athlete. Duke Henry, too, was both gifted intellectually and physically capable, 'delighted with riding and running in armour upon horseback'. It was no wonder that when a French embassy visited Edward's court in 1550 Duke Henry took part in a tournament of mixed teams of French and English knights, his side wearing yellow, their opponents blue, an observation the king did choose to record in his 'Chronicle'.[2]

Cheke's curriculum for the schoolroom looks formidable today. A ten-year-old boy had to work through Roman writers like Cicero, commit to memory passages of Latin and then translate them first into English and then back into Latin again. Edward's exercise books show us that he was diligent in applying himself to the kind of education that had made the best scholars of a generation.

Cheke was an inspiring teacher and a constant for Edward in all the busyness, the fun and the formality of court, a fixed point in his life. Roger Ascham remembered Cheke's words:

I would have a good student pass and journey through all authors both Greek and Latin. But he that will dwell in these few books only, first, in God's Holy Bible, and then join with it Tully [Cicero] in Latin, Plato, Aristotle, Xenophon, Isocrates and Demosthenes in Greek, must needs prove an excellent man.

Cheke's task was to shape Edward's mind and indeed his whole moral attitude. The kingdom would have a philosopher prince whose values were rooted in God, in learning and in chivalry.[3]

The greatest of all texts on public service was the *Offices* (*De Officiis*) of the great Roman politician and orator Cicero. With Cheke Edward worked carefully through its first and second books with no short cuts and no skim-reading. Edward practised his handwriting with Ascham, the best English penman of his generation, specially recruited for the task by Cheke. Together Ascham and the king worked to the models set out in the copybook on the roman hand written by the Italian scholar Giovanni Battista Palatino.

These exercises with Ascham tested Edward's precision and eye for detail. To form the letters perfectly each movement of his pen had to be just right: he had to use care and self-discipline. It was the kind of rigour a king needed to practise: to find the time and the patience to do his duty properly, to apply himself, his mind always on God. Edward's lessons with Ascham would have brought some moments of peace and stillness to the Privy Chamber, for it was impossible to write like Ascham, Cheke, Palatino or any other master of penmanship without being able to find a quiet and undisturbed place to work.

This was close and private time in Edward's inner rooms, so we are very lucky to have a few words by Ascham that give us an idea of how they talked to each other. Ascham wrote: 'his grace would oft most gently promise me, one day to do me good, and I would say, "Nay, your majesty will soon forget me when I shall be absent from you." Which thing, he said, he would never do.'

Ascham continued: 'I do not mistrust these words because they were spoken of a child, but rather I have laid up my sure hope in them because they were uttered by a king.' Edward was both a boy and a king: young, as impressionable as he was intelligent, still at barely ten years of age learning so much about the world. He lived in the bubble of court and majesty, where it was easy to trust the good intentions of those around him when they appeared to serve him loyally.[4]

The children of Henry VIII were not naive: political experience came to them early in life. In February 1548 Princess Elizabeth sent to her brother some lines in Latin that, when we realize that Elizabeth was fourteen when she wrote them, are breathtakingly revealing: 'it is ... rather characteristic of my nature not only not to say in words as much as I think in my mind, but also, indeed, not to say more than I think.' In that same letter she punned on two words in Greek, *kólakas* (flatterers) and *kórakas* (crows). Kings, Elizabeth wrote, should not appear to have 'more flatterers within their chambers than crows outside their court'.[5]

Edward's first experience of the tough politics of power at the Tudor court came with the Seymour affair in 1547 and 1548. He was eleven years old when it ended. It showed how, for all the security of his court, he was still vulnerable to the influence of an uncle. It gives us also a wonderful chance to hear the voices of men close to the king.

Thomas, Lord Seymour of Sudeley was the younger

brother of Protector Somerset. In 1547 he was about forty years of age, unmarried and, though not possessed of any great talent, the lord admiral of Edward's navy. But Thomas Seymour wanted more: he wanted to be his royal nephew's Governor. He wanted power and standing, and he was willing to try to manipulate the king's servants at court, and even Edward himself, in order to achieve his ambitions. He failed, and the price he paid for that failure was his life.

Thomas Seymour was experienced enough in the ways of a royal court to know that to get to the king he needed to befriend Edward's servants. He was himself a gentleman of the Privy Chamber and this gave him valuable access to the private suite of rooms around his nephew. When Edward's court was at St James's Palace in June 1547 Lord Seymour called in to see one of the king's grooms, John Fowler. Perhaps Fowler was sympathetic to Lord Seymour, who had the ability to rub along nicely with many people. Probably too, Fowler was flattered by his lordship's attentions. With hindsight he was very naive.

Fowler later recalled the words of their conversation that day at St James's. The exchange began something like this:

Seymour: Master Fowler, how doth the king's majesty?
Fowler: Well, thanks be to God.

Very quickly their conversation took a rather elliptical turn. Seymour asked if the king 'lacked anything', to which Fowler replied 'No'. Then he asked Fowler if the king 'would not in his absence ask for him, or ask any question of him'. Fowler answered that Edward 'would ask sometime for him but nothing else'. We can imagine Fowler wondering to himself at this point what on earth Seymour was driving at.

> *Fowler*: What question should the king ask of you?
> *Seymour*: Nay, nothing, unless sometime he would ask, why I married not.
> *Fowler*: Then I never heard him ask no such questions.

There was a pause; and then Seymour said:

> Master Fowler, I pray you, if you have any communication with the king's majesty soon or tomorrow, ask his highness whether he would be content I should marry or not. And if he say yea, I pray you ask his grace who he would should [*sic*] be my wife.

Fowler agreed.

And so that night, when Edward was alone, Fowler said to the king: 'If it please your grace, I marvel that my lord admiral marrieth not.' Edward said nothing, so Fowler pressed on: 'Could your grace be contented he should marry?' The king said 'very well'. Whom, Fowler asked Edward, would his grace choose to marry Lord Seymour? Edward said at first, 'My Lady Anne of Cleves', his father's fourth wife, by then thirty-one years old and living in unhappy retirement in Kent. But then the king paused and said: 'Nay, nay, wot you what [do you know what?] I would he married my sister [Princess] Mary to turn her [Catholic] opinions.' That was the end of their conversation: and a very peculiar one it had been.

Lord Seymour came to St James's next day and met

Fowler in the king's gallery. The admiral called Fowler over and asked him if he had done what he had been asked to do. Fowler said yes, and then told Seymour exactly what his nephew had said. Seymour laughed. He was silent for a little while. But then he said: 'I pray you, Master Fowler, if you may soon ask his grace if he could be content that I should marry the queen [Queen Katherine].' Would Fowler be a suitor for the admiral, and ask Edward to write a letter to Katherine? Fowler said that he would and spoke to the king about it that night.[6]

The following day Seymour came once again to the palace and had a private audience with Edward. Fowler wrote in a deposition a few months later that he had no idea what they talked about. But he hinted pretty strongly that a letter by Edward to Queen Katherine proposing the marriage between the queen and the admiral, though the work of the king, was written under Seymour's guidance. Seymour himself delivered Katherine's reply to Edward.

This was all a shadow play. Thomas Seymour and Queen Katherine had in fact already married. What Seymour believed he had got from the king was his blessing for a secret marriage that, once made public, would cause a huge political fuss. But Thomas Seymour had done more even than this, getting so close to the king that Edward had written a letter on his uncle's behalf and signed it 'Edward R', a teasing promise of power and patronage. A man as ambitious as Lord Seymour saw the possibilities.

And so Seymour played his hand at court, knowing whom to confide in, whom to get on his side: John Fowler, Sir Thomas Wroth and John Cheke of the Privy Chamber.

He often spoke to Fowler over a drink in the privy buttery. Always he asked the same question: what had the king said about him?

Now Seymour was beginning to say out loud things that a wiser man would have kept to himself. Once he even suggested how easy it might be to take the king by force. At nine o'clock one morning Seymour came into the king's gallery at St James's, where Fowler was playing his lute. Early on a summer's day, the court was unusually quiet. He greeted Fowler with a 'good morrow':

> *Seymour*: Here is slender company about the king. I
> came through the chamber of presence and found not
> a man, nor in all the house as I came I found not a
> dozen persons.
> *Fowler*: Thanks be to God we are in a quiet realm and
> the king's majesty is well beloved; if it were not so a
> hundred men would make foul work here.

Fowler remembered the words of Seymour's reply: 'A man might steal away the king now, for there came more with me than is in all the house besides.' And then he went to spend the morning privately with his nephew.[7]

In the course of eighteen months Thomas Seymour had secretly married the queen, tried to corrupt the king's servants, given money to Edward, attempted to use his nephew to manipulate a parliament and recruited some of the most important noblemen in England to support his pretensions. He even made predatory sexual advances on Princess Elizabeth. At the beginning of 1549 the whole affair was blown wide open and exposed in the kind of excruciating detail we are used to today in those great inquiries that bring to public scrutiny communications their authors never imagined would be read by curious outsiders. So many people were complicit in the affair, keeping private Seymour's overtures and indiscretions. Some of the greatest names in England must have squirmed as they gave their evidence to the king's secretaries.

Two men close to Edward left particularly exposed by the Seymour affair were John Fowler and John Cheke. Cheke knew exactly what Lord Seymour was up to and how dangerous he was. Once Seymour had come to him at Whitehall Palace 'with a piece of paper in his hand', saying that he had a suit for Parliament and that the king was 'well contented' to endorse it. He wanted Cheke to give it personally to Edward. Cheke remembered the words written on that piece of paper, in Seymour's handwriting: 'My lords, I pray you favour my lord admiral mine uncle's suit, which he will make unto you.' It was in effect a blank cheque for whatever Seymour chose to draw on it. All it needed was Edward's sign manual. Cheke told Seymour that the Duke of Somerset had commanded that the king should sign no document that he as Protector had not already countersigned. Cheke said to Seymour: 'I durst not be so bold to deliver it, nor to cause the king's majesty either to write it or else to set his hand unto it.' Seymour pressed him: after all, he said, he had the king's permission. But Cheke stood his ground, 'earnestly' refusing to accept from Seymour the piece of paper.[8]

In all the twists and turns of the Seymour affair the most important person was a ten-year-old king, a child at the centre of a world he did not yet fully understand, used and manipulated by an ambitious uncle. It is easy to be carried away by the grand words and great aspirations of kingly authority, but the fact is that Edward was vulnerable politically, physically and even emotionally.

The most extraordinary deposition in the Seymour affair is Edward's own. It tells us so much about a king still growing up, about his intelligence and acuity just as much as his innocence. In this document we really hear the words of a young king, speaking for himself to his uncle, taking the advice of John Cheke, and being encouraged to stand up for himself. We see, too, Seymour's cunning in playing on the vulnerabilities of Edward and his court: a king given pocket money by the chief gentleman of his Privy Chamber, a boy whose bluntness ('It were better that he should die') was surely to do with his youth and inexperience. Seymour had a talent for making others complicit in his power game – Fowler in effect his agent at court, Cheke and even a binder of the king's books used to get money secretly from the admiral to his nephew. This is how Edward explained it:

> The lord admiral came to me in the time of the last parliament at Westminster, and desired me to write a thing for him. I asked him what: he said it was none ill thing, it is for the queen's majesty. I said if it were good, the lords would allow it; if it were ill, I would not write in it. Then he said they would take it in better part if I would write. I desired him to let me alone in that matter. Cheke said afterwards to me 'Ye were not best to write'.

At another time within this two year at least, he said, 'Ye must take upon you yourself to rule, for ye shall be able enough as well as other kings; and then ye may give your men somewhat; for your uncle is old, and I trust will not live long.' I answered, 'It were better that he should die.' Then he said, 'Ye are but even a very beggarly king now, ye have not to play or to give to your servants.' I said, 'Master Stanhope had for me.' Then he said, he would give Fowler money for me, and so he did, as Fowler told me. And he gave Cheke money, as I bade him; and also to a bookbinder, as [Jean] Belmaine can tell; and to divers others at that time, I remember not to whom.

Fowler had praised Seymour, saying to Edward: 'Ye must thank my lord admiral for [the] gentleness that he showed you, and for his money.'

The admiral pressed Edward to be a king. His nephew was 'too bashful'. Why did he not want 'to bear rule, as other kings do'? Edward's reply was that of a boy still so much in the shadow of men: 'I said, I need not, for I was well enough.'[9]

4
'Methinks I am in prison'

Edward's stepmother the queen fell pregnant in December 1547. The following June, a few days before Katherine's confinement, Thomas Seymour wrote to her. They were the words of an expectant father and an embittered courtier: 'I hear my little man doth shake his head, trusting, if God should give him life to live as long as his father, he will revenge such wrongs as neither you nor I can at this present.' Lord Seymour had made his case to his brother the Protector: 'although I am in no hope ... yet am I in no despair'.[1]

The 'little man' was a girl, baptized Mary, who was born on 30 August 1548. Katherine developed puerperal fever and she died less than a week later, leaving all of her possessions to her husband. They did him little good.

Attainted by Parliament for offences within the compass of high treason, Thomas Seymour was beheaded on Tower Hill on 20 March 1549. In his 'Chronicle' Edward made a short and simple entry: 'the Lord Sudeley, admiral of England, was condemned to death and died the March ensuing.' Here there was no emotion and no obvious regret. Certainly there was no mention by Edward that it took two blows of the axe to remove his uncle's head. Was the king too shocked by Seymour's execution to write very much about it? Did he merely accept what had to be done? Did he simply feel nothing at all, a king who was also a boy blocking out emotion? Or was he just too young properly to understand it? All we know is that the entries nearby in the 'Chronicle' suggest Edward was much more interested in the English military hardware then rumbling through Scotland.[2]

Really only Bishop Hugh Latimer could have reflected so plainly upon the lord admiral. Preaching before the king and his courtiers within weeks of Seymour's execution, Latimer offered a flint-sharp meditation on God, culpability and redemption on the scaffold. If Latimer's words have the power to make us shudder today, revisiting as they do the blows of the headsman's axe, we can only imagine their effect upon those of his audience who had been caught up in Lord Seymour's terrible fall:

> What God can do, I can tell. I will not deny but that he may in the twinkling of an eye save a man and turn his heart. What he did [for Thomas Seymour] I cannot tell. And when a man hath two strokes with an axe, who can tell that between two strokes he doth repent? It is very hard to judge. Well, I will not go so nigh to work, but this I will say, if they ask me what I think of his death: that he died very dangerously, irksomely, horribly.

The Seymour affair caused Bishop Latimer and others to reflect on their boy king and his virtues. Was royal minority a curse on England? God, Latimer said, had before punished kingdoms 'whose ruler is a child' and where officials were always 'climbing and gleaning, stirring, searching and scraping and voluptuously set on banqueting'. But England, Latimer reassured his audience, was different. True, Edward was young, but he had 'as sage a Council as ever was in England' to help and advise him. To courtiers bruised by the Seymour affair Bishop Latimer offered hope, praising the king and his people. He said that God had blessed England with a noble young king who was being brought up by 'such schoolmasters as cannot be gotten in all the realm again', words that must have offered some comfort to John Cheke.[3]

Hugh Latimer saw in his mind's eye a peaceful and secure England. The political reality, however, was much more complicated. A few months after Latimer preached at Whitehall Palace, a rebellion broke out across the country. A few months after that Edward's court and government were turned upside down by Protector Somerset's fall from power, when King Edward was caught up in what was more or less a coup d'état.

If England, from the preaching place in Whitehall Palace, was to Bishop Latimer a peaceful and stable country, the view from inside the chamber of Edward's Privy Council was a radically different one.

Edward's kingdom was beset by some serious problems. It was stretched and under strain, weak internally and threatened by real and probable enemies. In April 1549 Sir William Paget, the king's secretary and Protector Somerset's most experienced adviser, wrote a frank report for the council on the condition of England and the standing of its diplomacy. Paget, as plain a man in politics as Latimer was in the pulpit, pulled no punches. The king's exchequer was burdened by debt and the kingdom had neither the money nor the experienced commanders and men to fight a war. He believed that the common people were restless, 'too liberal in speech, too bold and licentious in their doings and too wise and well learned in their own conceits'. Paget continued: 'All things in manner going backward and unfortunately and every man almost out of heart and courage, and our lacks so well known as our enemies despise us and our friends pity us.'[4]

This was more than a crisis of policy. Somerset's protectorship was barely holding together. In private, in May 1549, Paget pleaded with the duke to moderate his increasingly authoritarian behaviour. Even Sir William had felt Somerset's 'nips', though he hardly seemed to take these personally. But Paget was blunt. The Protector had to change his whole style of governing: 'I beseech you, and for God's sake, to consider and weigh well ... when the whole Council shall move you or give you advice in a matter ... to follow the same and to relent sometime from your opinion.' He appealed to Somerset to act for God's glory, the king's honour, and his own surety and protection. Somerset ignored him. Paget later described himself as Cassandra, the prophetess who foresaw the destruction of Troy but was believed by no one.[5]

The crisis came in the summer of 1549. Edward, by now eleven years old, knew what was happening. The cumulative rumble of disaster was clear from the wonderfully concise entries he made in his 'Chronicle':

> The people began to rise in Wiltshire ... Then they rose in Sussex, Hampshire, Kent, Gloucestershire, Suffolk, Warwickshire, Essex, Hertfordshire, a piece of Leicestershire, Worcestershire, and Rutlandshire ... After that they rose in Oxfordshire, Devonshire, Norfolk and Yorkshire.

Uprisings throughout the kingdom were shaking pretty much the whole of England. And Paget's predictions were becoming horribly real. King Henri II of France took advantage of Protector Somerset's weakness to attack English-held Boulogne. There were rumours in July that Edward was dead, and to squash them he rode publicly through London. Days earlier Paget had urged Somerset to deal with the rebels more vigorously than he had done so far. Force and justice were needed to keep subjects in order. But Somerset appeared to wobble, even to conciliate the rebels. Councillors went out to confront dangerous rebel armies in Norfolk and the West Country, where there was some sharp fighting.[6]

The rebellion was a conflation of many grievances. In two years there had been huge changes in religion and worship. The altars, religious stained glass and statues of Catholic England had been broken down by zealous Protestant reform. English men and women now worshipped with an English Prayer Book. Change had come from the top, led by Archbishop Cranmer and Protector Somerset. There were deep worries too over a precarious economy.

Always lurking was the question of Edward's minority

and how far a boy king was being misled by courtiers out to line their own purses. So Protector Somerset's government threw everything it could at defending the king and his kingship, putting out a robustly written pamphlet on the authority of King Edward and his Reformation: 'You are our subjects because we be your king, and rule we will, because God hath willed: it is as great a fault in us, not to rule, as in a subject not to obey.' This was Edward's voice, though it is highly unlikely that the words were his own: every monarch's public pronouncements were most often the work of his or her officials. Archbishop Cranmer preached on the absolute obedience demanded of all subjects. Rebels went to hell for blasphemy against God and king. Even John Cheke was recruited to write a pamphlet against rebellion in which he defended with vigour the authority of the king and his laws. For Cheke the rebels had threatened to tear apart the whole social order, to turn the world upside down with great 'uproars of people, hurly burlies of vagabonds, routs of robbers'.[7]

In October the Duke of Somerset's protectorate fell to pieces. His colleagues in the council simply refused any longer to accept his authority; his credibility was spent. Paget's analysis had been correct: Edward Seymour had broken the trust given to him as Protector. At last Sir William's Cassandra had to be believed. The policies Somerset had pushed and pressed in council against the advice even of Paget had failed.

In the course of a few days everything changed. In what turned out to be a fantastic misjudgement, Edward Seymour seized the king and took him from Hampton Court to the security of Windsor Castle. A week later the Duke of Somerset was under heavy guard in the Tower of London. Edward, once again, was at the centre of things: this time it was a rushed and confused effort at a coup d'état.

Edward himself told the story of what had happened in his 'Chronicle'. He wrote:

> The Council, about 19 of them, were gathered in London, thinking to meet with the Lord Protector, and to make him amend some of his disorders. He, fearing his state, caused the secretary [Sir William Petre] in my name to be sent to the lords, to know for what cause they gathered their powers together, and if they meant to talk with him, that they should come in peaceable manner.

On 6 October Protector Somerset called for the support of the people and ordered the defence of Hampton Court. At nine or ten o'clock that night he took the king to Windsor Castle.[8]

For days messengers and emissaries went to and from Windsor and London carrying some very sharp exchanges of words between Somerset and the council. Both sides issued proclamations in the name of the king. The council suspected Somerset of inciting the common people to arms. There were accusations and counter-accusations of treason.

What makes Edward a mystery in Somerset's misadventure is his silence. In the 'Chronicle' he said really nothing at all about what actually happened at Hampton Court and Windsor. He gave no fly-on-the-wall account of Somerset's actions. How did Somerset justify to his nephew what he had done? How did he plan and execute the remove to Windsor Castle? What was his mood like? Was Edward at any time afraid? All we have are the bare facts: that Somerset whisked the king off to Windsor at night time in chilly October, and that the duke said he was ready to use armed force to defend the castle against any attack.

If Edward's silence is dignified and kingly, it is also hugely frustrating. It means that we have to fill in the gaps for ourselves, making certain assumptions about what the king knew and understood. First, we know that Edward signed letters and documents which were countersigned by Somerset and then authenticated with the king's signet seal. Here Edward was involved in one of two ways. Either he signed blank sheets of paper for his uncle or he signed the finished documents. The first possibility seems unlikely: surely if the Seymour affair had taught him anything, it was the importance of his sign manual and the power of those seven letters written by his own hand – 'Edward R'. Probably Edward was presented with the completed documents, which means we can assume (even if we cannot know for certain) that he had a fair idea of how Somerset was appealing for help and support and justifying his position in taking the king. Once again, young Edward was being pulled along by family loyalty.

Perhaps what convinced Edward most of all of Somerset's goodwill and honesty was the presence at Windsor of two other men who had always watched over him as prince and king. They were Archbishop Cranmer, the man Edward called his guardian and father, and the deeply experienced Sir William Paget. Cranmer and Paget offered their support to the Protector, but they were also able to begin something like a reasonable dialogue with the council in London. Cranmer had moral weight and authority: Paget's skill was an instinctive grasp of tricky diplomacy. If Somerset had been on his own at Windsor, uncounselled and unrestrained, the whole episode might have ended much more bloodily than it eventually did.

On 8 October a letter of reconciliation was sent to the council in London: it was in Edward's name with his sign manual at the top. Not surprisingly, it suggested the king's sympathy for the duke. Edward and his advisers at Windsor had found the duke so 'tractable' that he and they were sure that a peaceful agreement could be found by the two sides. What follows sounds like the voice of a very young king refined by the tact and experience of Cranmer and Paget:

> We verily believe, and so do you we dare say, that he mind no hurt; if in government he hath not so discreetly used himself as in your opinions he might have done, we think the extremity in such a case is not to be acquired at his hand. Yet it lieth in us to remit it. For he is our uncle whom you know we love.[9]

But the council in London was unmoved. In fact it stood firmer than ever. The following day a letter was drafted for both Princess Mary and Princess Elizabeth to offer evidence of Somerset's treason. Most shocking of all was what they alleged Somerset had said publicly at Hampton Court before he went to Windsor, going so far as to claim that he made a threat to kill the king: '"here he is", quoth he, pointing to the king's majesty, "that shall die before me" – the most abominable saying that ever passed mouth of a subject towards his prince and sovereign.'[10]

So the council's position even after Edward's letter was just as robust and challenging as it had been before it. Perhaps the councillors saw Somerset weakening; perhaps they knew that to win – and to survive too – they had to press harder than ever their own authority. They wrote to the king himself on 9 October, replying to his letter of the day before. Not surprisingly they took great care in drafting it and made sure to keep a properly registered copy in the council's book.

With his own eyes Edward had seen Thomas Seymour fall. He had listened to Hugh Latimer preaching at Whitehall on the power he held from God to rule his subjects. He had recorded the spasms of a great rebellion. He had been effectively kidnapped by the Duke of Somerset. Now the young king was given a short lesson in the already complicated constitutional history of his reign. The council explained that Somerset's powers were limited:

> The protectorship and governance of your most royal person was not granted him by your father's will but only by agreement first amongst us the executors and after of others; those titles and special trust was committed to him during your majesty's pleasure and upon condition he should do all things by advice of your Council.

Choosing to forget quite for how long they had accepted Somerset's princely authority, they stuck to their duties as executors of Henry VIII in the interests of the kingdom. Rarely can a young king have been forced to grow up so quickly.[11]

Two days later it was all over. Twenty-two councillors were at the sheriff of London's house to sign the letter to the king. Neither Cranmer nor Paget was going to support Somerset unconditionally. The council in London commanded the Tower and its arsenal. And Edward was beginning to feel like a prisoner.

So with very little fuss the Duke of Somerset more or less surrendered. On the morning of 11 October he was taken into custody by Sir Anthony Wingfield, the king's vice-chamberlain, and escorted to the Tower. Wingfield, with Archbishop Cranmer and Sir William Paget, later gave to the council a report of what he had done. Clearly he was taking no chances: the duke, he wrote, was now in the Lieutenant's Tower, 'a very high tower and a strong and good watch shall be had about the same'.

They found that Edward had a cold that had been brought on by the ride at night to Windsor Castle and 'the subtlety' of the October air. He was feeling cooped up. As he said to Wingfield: 'methinks I am in prison: here be no galleries nor no gardens to walk in.' But he seemed remarkably unaffected by a pretty bizarre episode in his life. In fact he was almost breezily cheerful, walking in after breakfast that day to wish Wingfield good morning. He sent his greetings to the council in London 'with a merry countenance and a loud voice'. The gentlemen with Wingfield kissed the king's hand, 'every one much to their comforts'. Cranmer, Paget and Wingfield signed their report with what must have been a huge sigh of relief. After a peculiar, fractious and difficult episode, for the king at least it was business as usual.[12]

Paget was already preparing for Edward's remove to Richmond Palace, but the king's physician wanted Edward to go instead either back to Hampton Court or to London. Presumably it was on his doctor's orders that the king went to Hampton Court where, within days, with Somerset safely in the Tower, the council restructured the court. Edward recorded what happened in his 'Chronicle': 'Afterward I came to Hampton Court where they appointed by my consent six lords of the Council to be attendant on me at least two, and four knights.' In other words, two of six lords and barons of the Privy Council would always be with the king, along with four other knights. All were experienced men and many of them had been successful soldiers. First the Seymour affair and then Somerset's coup: it was obvious now that there had to be better arrangements to keep Edward safe and well.[13]

The Duke of Somerset was simply removed from the political scene. Edward's account of the end of Somerset's protectorship makes it sound like the sort of straightforward voluntary retirement from power and office it most certainly was not: 'The Lord Protector by his own agreement and submission lost his protectorship, treasurership, marshalship, all his moveables, and near £2000 [of] land by act of parliament.'[14]

Edward's words were as crisp and precise as ever. Do they suggest that he was detached and a little remote? Probably they do, but this was appropriate for a king. Was he naive? Surely not, given everything that had happened to him between 1547 and 1549, and the clarity of his observations. Perhaps he remembered those words written by his sister Elizabeth in 1548.

Edward recorded much of what went on in his life in his 'Chronicle'. It was in the spring of 1550, when he was half a year away from his thirteenth birthday, that the 'Chronicle' really picks up in pace and detail and assumes a kind of literary form. So what is it and what can it tell us about a boy king quickly growing up?

The 'Chronicle' was an excellent training in observation, something like the exercise that was set for the fictional eleven-year-old Claudius (in later life Emperor of Rome) by his beloved tutor Athenodorus in Robert Graves's historical novel *I, Claudius*: 'he proposed to teach me not facts which I could pick up anywhere for myself, but the proper presentation of facts.' We will never really know, but it seems likely that John Cheke encouraged Edward to keep the 'Chronicle'. Certainly it allowed Edward to practise writing the kind of plain and robust English about which John Cheke was passionate.[15]

The 'Chronicle' was a working document. Much of it is rough and scrappy and falls a long way short of the beautiful penmanship and presentation of Cheke and Roger Ascham. Edward very likely kept it in a drawer of his private writing desk, a handsome piece of furniture covered with black velvet and decorated with plates of copper and gilt.

Edward loved objects and bric-a-brac. We know that his

desk was stuffed full of oddments: a brooch, buttons, coins, metal tags, an iron stamp, boxes for ink. And that is what his 'Chronicle' is like: precisely observed and expressed, but a magpie collection of facts, of happenings at court, the signing of foreign treaties, fragments of diplomatic reports, accounts of tournaments, details of military campaigns and equipment, reports of deaths. It is not a private diary: there is precious little in the 'Chronicle' of Edward's thoughts or feelings. Its style is more like one of the great Tudor chronicles of history, with events set out more or less in the order that they happened.

So the 'Chronicle' is not a kind of confessional. When we read that terse entry on the execution of Thomas Seymour we have to be careful not to make modern assumptions about how important it is to articulate and express our emotions; we can be certain that Edward was trained from a very early age to hide his feelings behind a mask of royalty, even in private and on paper.

And yet his 'Chronicle' can still tell us much about Edward. By the spring months of 1550 the impersonality of its opening pages on his life – that sense of a life looked at from the outside, in the third person – was quickly disappearing. Edward was now writing about himself as 'me' and 'I': a king active in the life of his kingdom, not someone merely passively in receipt of events.

Behind the mask of royalty and the emotional discipline of being a king, Edward was a boy – and a boy's boy at that. This becomes wonderfully clear when we read in the 'Chronicle' his account of a great naval display put on by Lord Clinton at Deptford in June 1550. Clinton was the

king's new lord admiral, an experienced soldier and a former governor of Boulogne who was promoted to the Privy
Council and admitted to Edward's Privy Chamber. Deptford was Clinton's celebration of his new importance in the
king's government.

The king loved every minute of the display: the soldiers
in their bright colours, the boats, the feigned combat, the
bangs and explosions and darts of fire, ending with the
heroic victory of the king's admiral in taking a mock castle
by force. Edward's description of what happened is bursting with a boy's enthusiasm for war and adventure, written
in clear, precise and vigorous prose that bubbles with his
excitement at what he was watching.

Here we find Edward in his element, a king of twelve and
a half who could not take his clear, grey eyes off what was
going on in front of him on the River Thames on a summer's evening after supper, held by this promise of action
and heroism. Here he was every inch the son of Henry VIII.

After supper was there a fort made upon a great lighter on
the Thames, which had three walls and a watchtower in the
midst of it . . . with forty or fifty other soldiers in yellow and
black. To the fort also appertained a galley of yellow colour
with men and munition in it for defence of the castle. Wherefore there came four pinnaces with their men in white
handsomely dressed, which, intending to give assault to the
castle, first drove away the yellow pinnace, and after with
clods, squibs, canes of fire, darts made for the nonce, and
bombards assaulted the castle; and at length came with their
pieces and burst the outer walls of the castle, beating them of

the castle into the second ward, who after issued out and drove away the pinnaces, sinking one of them, out of which all the men in it, being more than twenty, leaped out and swam in the Thames. Then came the admiral of the navy with three other pinnaces and won the castle by assault and burst the top of it down . . . Then the admiral went forth to take the yellow ship and at length clasped with her, took her, and assaulted also her top, and won it by composition and so returned home.[16]

5
'A challenge made by me'

The material reality of Edward VI's life was a physical and tangible one, of beautiful objects as well as rewards and obligations. It was a king's world of sport and recreation, of education and of religion, of learning to govern and of play and fun. The Privy Purse expenses recorded by his officials show us a lively and bustling court. Here are Edward's shirts and buttons, his bags of fragrant powders, his longbows and crossbows and his portable bed rich in cloth of gold, velvet and silk ribbon. We find payments to his majesty's apothecary, Thomas Alsopp, for stores of ginger candy water and to Thomas Browne, the king's cap-maker, 'for sundry cap feathers of sundry sorts and for trimming of divers caps and feathers together'.

There were rewards Edward made either in recognition of gifts or more generally out of his largesse. 'One that brought hawks' from a foreign duke was given £30 (today something over £6,000), while the servant of the Earl of Tyrone, who presented the king with two falcons and 'a brace of greyhounds', received £6. The servant of the genial diplomat Sir Philip Hoby who played to the king on the lute found himself a richer man by £10. There were gifts for many noblemen at the christenings of their children. Scholars who presented their works to Edward were rewarded by the scholar king: £30 for the renowned Dutch polymath Hadrianus Junius, £7 10s. for the Frenchman 'that gave his majesty a book in French of civil policy', and the great sum of £50 for Louis Le Roy, 'that gave the king's majesty Isocrates's orations translated into French' (Isocrates was an ancient Greek rhetorician whose work was specially commended by John Cheke). Some got money from the king because they were ill. Edward once sent £20 to the German Protestant theologian Martin Bucer, sick and miserable in freezing Cambridge.[1]

There was always music and song at Edward's court: John Fowler playing his lute at nine o'clock in the morning in the king's gallery at St James's; Sir Philip Hoby's man performing before the king; Peter and Philip van Wilder of the Privy Chamber doing the same. Philip took care of Edward's lutes, paid from the Privy Purse for 'lute strings and for ribbing and for lining his majesty's lute cases'. Edward listened to the voices of the six singing children of his Privy Chamber and his singing men. Other performers entertained the king, including the private players of the nobility, of the Duke of Somerset, of the dowager Duchess of Suffolk (the mother of Edward's companions Duke Henry and Lord Charles), and of the Marquess of Northampton. The king rewarded them all. During the great French embassy of 1551 some of the ambassador's men entertained the court on flutes and sackbuts, while one vaulted and danced on a rope and a boy 'tumbled before the king's majesty'.[2]

The life of any royal court was a performance, from the routine and familiar structures of the everyday to the elaborate shows of splendour and taste at Christmas and New

Year, at Shrovetide, and for the visits of foreign ambassadors. Sometimes Edward's court resembled the front and back stages of a West End show. Dramatic ambition was never wanting. At Hampton Court in 1547 players and torchbearers performed in a masque set around a 'counterfeit Tower of Babylon'. In 1549 the king and his courtiers were entertained by hermits, lance-men and friars, their costumes put together by the king's Revels Office: gold skins and silver paper, cloths of red and popinjay green, pilgrims' staves, canvas bags and globes. This was a riot of colour, music, performance and satire.[3]

At Christmas and New Year of 1550 and 1551 the Revels Office was especially busy. Its teams of joiners, carpenters and painters worked for days and nights to get everything ready for performances before the king and his courtiers. The tailors were busiest of all, fifteen of them, each paid for six days and two nights of work. The Revels Office operated under the watchful eye of its master, Sir Thomas Cawarden, and Cawarden answered directly to the Privy Council: entertainment at court was a serious business.

Twelfth Night in 1551 was celebrated at Greenwich Palace to the sound of an Irish bagpiper hired specially for the evening. The other performers were brought to the court by barge. There were Irishmen everywhere, or at least masquers dressed for the part, carrying 'Irish swords' and shields and between them a halberd. Canvas, flax, linen, Paris silk, coarse Paris thread, felts, sheepskin and lambskin, black thread and thread of 'divers colours', yellow gold sarsenet – we can almost reach out to touch the costumes for ourselves.[4]

The king paid seven 'players of interludes': Robert Hinstock, George Birch, Richard Coke, Richard Skinner, Henry Harriot, John Birch and Thomas Southey. We know that Will Somers, Edward's fool, performed that Twelfth Night. So probably did Edward and, given the Irish theme of the masque, his friend Barnaby Fitzpatrick too. The accounts of the Revels Office record the 'new making, translating, garnishing and finishing of divers and sundry garments, apparel, vestures and properties as well for the king's majesty in his person, as his young lords and divers players and other persons'. So as well as presenting at court serious orations in classical Greek and Latin under the eye of John Cheke, which by now Edward was doing on Sundays, the young king was a practised performer on the stage. Very likely it served him well in the great set-piece performances of his kingly duties.[5]

Cheke was as ever drilling Edward in his studies. The works of Cicero, that touchstone of Roman public duty, were never out of the schoolroom. As well as Latin and now Greek, Edward also kept up with the modern languages. Jean Belmaine continued as the king's French tutor, working with him at ever more sophisticated compositions. Louis Le Roy, who was a scholar of European reputation, made his presentation of Isocrates in French to the king in person in October 1550. Sir William Pickering, Edward's ambassador in Paris, sent to the king Louis Meigret's *Grammaire française*, as well as a popular book by the Spanish author Pedro Mexía. Edward read the dialogues in French and English published by Pierre Du Ploiche, a French Protestant refugee living and working in London. Du Ploiche's book was a kind of Berlitz phrasebook of its day, beginning with various prayers but mainly covering travel, food, buying and selling, numbers and the alphabet. Here eager students of modern French could search for phrases like 'God speed you sir' ('*Dieu vous gard monsieur*') or, for bedtime, 'Mine host, I have great lust to go to rest' ('*Mon hoste i'ay grant fain d'alter reposer*'). There are some wonderful set-piece conversations Edward is unlikely ever to have needed, including one on the absence of a wife sick with the ague for fifteen days or more. Another little scenario concerns a schoolboy far humbler than the king:

James, can you speak good French?
>Yea, a little sir.
Where go you to school?
>In Trinity Lane at the sign of the Rose.
Have you long time learned to speak French?
>Almost half a year.
Learn you also to write?
>Yea sir.
What more?
>The Latin tongue.
It is well done: learn always well.[6]

Edward's study of French went far beyond these conversational pleasantries, for under Belmaine's supervision he wrote essays on the weightier topics of religious idolatry, the Christian faith and the false supremacy of the pope.

Edward's education was for its day a broad one. Though rooted in the classical curriculum, he learned mathematics with the help of Robert Recorde's *Pathway to Knowledge* and a rare edition of Euclid's *Elements*. Recorde dedicated his book to the king, explaining the importance of a mathematical education:

> And for human knowledge this will I boldly say, that whosoever will attain true judgment therein, must not only travail [work hard] in the knowledge of the tongues, but must also before all other arts taste the mathematical sciences, specially arithmetic and geometry, without which it is not possible to attain full knowledge in any art.[7]

Edward loved astronomy. In his private study at Whitehall Palace there were six 'instruments of astronomy hanging upon the wall'. When in November 1549 the Privy Council sealed up the 'chair house' and secret jewel house at Whitehall (till then only the disgraced Protector Somerset had had the keys to them) Edward took away three astronomical instruments and gave one of them to his companion Lord Strange. What certainly survives is a brass horary quadrant very likely made for Edward by Thomas Gemini. Gemini was one of the king's surgeons but he was also a talented engraver and printer. The quadrant could be used to find the hour of the day, to mark the movements of the sun and moon, and to find the date of Easter. It is a beautiful object, inscribed with Gemini's initials and the name of the king, 'Edwardus Rex'. What Edward's other 'instruments' were we can guess: astrolabes, astronomical compendiums, ring sun dials, nocturnals. Here was the promise of discovering so much about the earth and the stars, as well as a world of navigation and travel – fascinating for any fourteen-year-old boy gripped as Edward was by adventure and action.[8]

More obscure – but in many ways more tantalizing still – are Edward's encounters with the writings of Niccolò Machiavelli. Here we meet the intriguing and elusive character of William Thomas, a clerk of Edward's Privy Council.

Once an apprentice on the run from his master, Thomas spent time in Italy, where he fell in love with the Italian dialects and the histories of the Italian city states. Power and government fascinated him. In 1549 and 1550 he had printed in London *The historie of Italie* and a book of political morality called *The vanitee of this world*. Thomas's *Principal rules of the Italian grammar* (1550) was the first Italian grammar and dictionary published in English. So the young man who had gone on the run to Italy made good in the end.[9]

Thomas dedicated *The historie of Italie* to John Dudley, Earl of Warwick, by then the most powerful of the king's councillors. With a canny eye for further patronage, he presented a work of translation to Edward's companion Henry, Duke of Suffolk, and gave the king a New Year's gift of an account of Venetian voyages to the Middle East. Here Thomas wrote glowingly of England, whose subjects were 'the king's children and not slaves as they be otherwhere'. He presented his translation to Edward knowing that the young king was 'most desirous of all virtuous knowledge'.[10]

Thomas had boundless confidence in his own ability. He was never likely to sit quietly in the Privy Council office and be wholly satisfied at keeping the council's register up to date or writing the councillors' letters. He was bursting with knowledge he wanted to impart. Not someone with easy access to the king's private rooms, Thomas devised a clever way of communicating with Edward. When he gave the council's papers to Sir Nicholas Throckmorton of the Privy Chamber for the king to read, he included with them some essays of his own. Thomas felt there was no more deserving recipient than Edward of everything he knew about politics, Italy, statecraft and government reform.

In this way Thomas introduced the king to the writings of Machiavelli, using them to discuss interesting topics about government with a young king whose knowledge was growing all the time. Thomas never used Machiavelli's name: here he was at his most ebullient, with (as one historian once wrote) 'a sense of humour beyond the ordinary' and a Renaissance scholar's talent for plagiarism.[11]

Thomas had read Machiavelli's *History of Florence* in order to write *The historie of Italie*: 'Nicolas Macchiavegli, a notable learned man, and secretary of late days to the commonwealth there'. What Thomas supplied to Edward was not *The Prince*, that extraordinary analysis of political power; instead it was Machiavelli's greatest work, his account of republican government called *The Discourses*, on the first ten books of Livy's *History of Rome*. Three of Thomas's 'discourses' for Edward survive: on whether it is best to adapt policy to changing times; on the friendship of princes; and on whether the power in a state should rest in the nobility or in the common people. Thomas also wrote a paper for Edward on the reform of England's coinage, showing here that he had an eye for a topic that interested the king. Edward seems to have enjoyed unpicking technical subjects like currency, international trade and military campaigns of history.[12]

And so in this way young Edward VI learned his Machiavelli, mediated through the lively mind and busy pen of

Master William Thomas. It was a mild but also a stimulating dose, and it played both to the political and intellectual passions of Thomas and to Edward's education by John Cheke in the ancient historians. Thomas's discourses spoke to a young king who was beginning to see the political world around him through an ever more sophisticated lens. The bright boy of fourteen was very different from the king of nine or ten.

Like so much of Edward's life there is a lot that we will never know. We can guess that Thomas and his king met only rarely. Thomas's essays for Edward from Machiavelli were a secret. Thomas wrote:

> It becometh a prince for his wisdom to be had in admiration
> . . . And since nothing serveth more to that than to keep the
> principal things of wisdom secret till occasion require the
> utterance, I would wish them to be kept secret. Referring it
> nevertheless to your majesty's good will and pleasure.[13]

Perhaps Edward squirrelled Thomas's papers away in his writing desk, along with his 'Chronicle' and the bric-a-brac – as private a space as a young king was ever likely to have.

In the spring and summer of 1551 Edward was absorbed by competitive archery. In his 'Chronicle' for 31 March he wrote: 'A challenge made by me that I, with sixteen of my Chamber, should run at base, shoot, and run at ring with any seventeen of my servants, gentlemen in the court.' These were the skills of combat at which his father had excelled: running, archery, and riding on horseback with a lance. The following day the competition began: 'The first day of the challenge at base, or running, the king won.' Five days later he lost 'at rounds' (shooting at targets set at a fixed distance from the archer) but won at 'rovers' (shooting at targets selected at random). His competitive appetite was beginning to sharpen.[14]

All the time he was moving towards manhood. So in May and June, with Edward by now thirteen years of age, there was a flurry of diplomatic activity, with first Sir Philip Hoby, then the Bishop of Ely and finally the Marquess of Northampton sent off to France to negotiate Edward's marriage to Elizabeth, the six-year-old daughter of King Henri II. Henri was serious enough about the prospective match to present Edward with her portrait. Hoby went with ten gentlemen dressed in velvet and wearing chains of gold. Northampton was the principal ambassador, whose task it was first to present Henri with the Order of the Garter and then to negotiate the terms for the marriage. Edward's government expected Elizabeth to bring with her a marriage portion of 12,000 marks a year and the staggering dowry of at least 800,000 French crowns. Edward's treasury would forfeit 100,000 crowns if he failed to perform the agreement.

A month later France reciprocated with an embassy. Where King Henri had been made a Knight of the Garter, so Edward would be elected to the correspondingly elite Order of St Michael. Henri's ambassador, Jacques d'Albon, Marquis de Fronsac, Seigneur de St-André, left Châteaubriant for England on 11 June with a train of up to five hundred horse and the best of King Henri's musicians. It was obvious that Edward's court would have to put on quite a show to receive them.

Edward accepted the Order of St Michael 'by promise' to the French ambassador resident at his court on 16 June. Four days later Northampton, by now in France, invested Henri with the Garter in the king's bedchamber. With great formality the Bishop of Ely made an oration to which the Cardinal of Lorraine replied. A day later they got down to business. Edward recorded in his 'Chronicle' that the French commissioners 'did most cheerfully assent' to his marriage to Elizabeth, agreeing with Northampton that neither party should be bound either in conscience or in honour until she was at least twelve years of age. But the French mocked the sums of money asked of Henri by Edward's diplomats. By Edward's account it took four days for the commissioners to hammer out an agreement satisfactory to both sides. Successful French haggling brought the dowry down to 200,000 crowns, to which Edward's negotiators agreed so long as Elizabeth was eventually brought to England at Henri's expense.[15]

Edward told much of the story of the embassy of the Maréchal de St-André in his 'Chronicle'. Right from the beginning the diplomatic and royal etiquette had to be impeccable. When St-André arrived at the port of Rye he was met by a royal official who presented him with Edward's handwritten letters and made arrangements for the baggage of the ambassador's great entourage to be carried up to London. St-André was feasted by courtiers on the journey to meet Edward. In London a merciless sweating sickness had broken out that, in the king's understanding, killed its victims within three hours and caused some to 'die raving'. This was the sweat that, when it reached Cambridge, killed Edward's companions Henry, Duke of Suffolk and his brother Lord Charles. On the day St-André arrived in London a gentleman of the King's Chamber and a groom died. Quickly Edward was removed for safety to Hampton Court.[16]

St-André was welcomed to London by the sound of the cannon of fifty warships in the Thames and the ordnance of the Tower of London. To escape the infection he went to Richmond Palace. His embassy was huge: Edward was told that St-André had with him about four hundred gentlemen. The following morning, 14 July, the maréchal came to meet the king. Edward described the occasion with a precise eye for diplomatic protocol and a keen memory:

> He came to me at Hampton Court at nine of the clock ... and so conveyed first to me, where, after his master's recommendations and letters, he went to his chamber ... all hanged with cloth of arras, and so was the hall and all my lodging. He dined with me also. After dinner, being brought into an inner chamber, he told me he was come not only for delivery of the Order but also for to declare the great friendship the king his master bore me, which he desired I would think to be such to me as a father beareth to his son, or brother to brother ... I answered him that I thanked him for his Order and also his love, etc. and I would show like love in all points.

The next day St-André formally invested Edward with the Order of St Michael.[17]

Edward seems to have thoroughly enjoyed himself during the embassy. There were grand dinners of a dozen courses in great outdoor banqueting houses built in Hyde Park and Marylebone Park. The structure in Hyde Park was especially splendid, with stairs, a turret, ranges built of brick and furnaces for boiling water, and tables, trestles and dressers. Edward wrote that St-André saw a display of 'the strength of the English archers', and the king and the maréchal and their gentlemen hunted together. There were gifts and rewards, including for St-André a diamond ring from Edward's finger 'both for [the maréchal's] pains and also for my memory'. The rewards of money were huge: £3,000 in gold for the maréchal and sums of £1,000 and £500 for the other senior diplomats in the embassy.

Most interesting of all was the private time that Edward and St-André spent together. On 20 July the maréchal saw the king on a typical day in his life. Edward wrote:

> He came to see mine arraying [dressing] and saw my bedchamber and went a-hunting with hounds and saw me shoot and saw all my guard shoot together. He dined with me, heard me play on the lute, ride, came to me in my study, supped with me, and so departed to Richmond.

Here was Edward's world in his private rooms, perhaps with Philip van Wilder carrying his lute, John Cheke and Edward's officials in the king's study, the gentlemen and grooms of the Privy Chamber always in attendance, exercising, studying, eating, conversing: a king for whom there was all the promise of the future – adulthood, marriage, a realm to be governed by a young man who was to his fingertips a prince, and a dynastic union between England and

France that would surely shape the future of the whole of Europe.[18]

This promise is shown most beautifully in a portrait of the king now in the Musée du Louvre in Paris. It was painted in 1551 by Edward's court artist Guillim Scrots, and probably it was the picture referred to by Edward's resident ambassador at the French court, Sir William Pickering, in October of that year. Flattering Edward, King Henri had told Pickering that the picture 'was very excellent and that the natural [that is, Edward in the flesh] as he was persuaded much exceeded the artificial'.[19]

Scrots painted Edward in full length, a very conscious nod to the style of portraiture favoured by the powerful Habsburgs of the Holy Roman Empire: Edward was a king to be reckoned with, easily equal to his brother monarchs of Europe, just as his father had been. He is beautifully dressed in a doublet of brown intricately patterned in gold thread and decorated with golden aglets. In his right hand are gloves. The thumb and fingers of his left hand hold the belt of his richly decorated rapier. On his chest is the Garter medallion of St George, the viewer's eyes drawn to its handsome broad blue ribbon around his neck.

Scrots's Edward has lost the immaturity of the portrait of 1546. The young boy is now very much the adolescent of fourteen. Still the pale skin, the grey, steady eyes and the auburn hair: but Edward's face is slim and his jawline more defined than it was as prince.

Here was the acknowledged and legitimate heir to the throne of Henry VIII: here was England's hope for the future.

6

'My device for the succession'

The New Year of 1553 was celebrated at Edward's court with the satire of the Lord of Misrule, George Ferrers, Master of the King's Pastimes. Misrule was an entertainer and an impresario, a subverter of the accepted order of things who poked fun at the formal and serious world of the king and his government precisely in order to celebrate it.

Ferrers planned his entertainments with extraordinary care, like a general setting out every manoeuvre before a battle. He sent an embassy to Edward to prepare the court for the arrival at Greenwich Palace of a whole royal entourage: councillors, a theologian, a philosopher, a poet, a physician, an apothecary, a master of requests, a lawyer, gentlemen ushers, fools, jugglers, tumblers and friars. Ferrers arranged a tournament of twelve hobby horses, with half of Misrule's troupe dressed in white and blue and the others in black and yellow. On Twelfth Night, 5 January, Ferrers and his players performed 'A triumph or play of Cupid'. A small boy played Cupid, 'clad in a canvas hose and doublet silvered over, with a pair of wings in gold, with bow and arrows, his eyes bended'. The goddess Venus appeared with a masque of ladies and the god Mars came in 'very triumphantly'.

Misrule's reign came to an end on Twelfth Night, but the Revels Office then began straight away to prepare for Candlemas and Shrovetide, with entertainments of Greek worthies and Medioxes ('being half death, half man'), of bagpipes, cats, and tumblers 'going upon their hands with their feet upward', with a play on Ireland 'and divers other plays and pastimes'. They all sound wonderfully exotic.[1]

And they were the last entertainments that Edward ever saw. 1553, which had arrived in such style thanks to George Ferrers, was the year of the young king's death: the year Henry VIII's precious jewel was taken from his people and when England felt the sting of God's terrible judgement.

Acts of providence that shake whole countries can begin in very small ways. Edward caught a bad cold, which by February had become a fever that confined him to his chamber and meant that the masques and plays had to be postponed. The cold lingered into March, but he was feeling better by April. On the 11th Edward removed from Whitehall to Greenwich; the royal barge was saluted by the cannon of the Tower of London. He was well enough four days later to attend to some official papers. But he was weak and had a nagging cough.

In London rumours began to circulate that Edward was dying. In the first week of May one man had his ear nailed to the pillory on Cheapside and two women were punished outside Whitehall Palace. All three wore a placard that read: 'For most false and untrue reports touching the king's majesty's life.' Other Londoners gossiped about the king and the predatory ambitions of his most powerful adviser, John Dudley, Duke of Northumberland.[2]

In early May Edward's health appeared to improve. Sir William Petre, one of his secretaries, even reported that the king was 'very well amended'. But by the end of the month Edward was seriously ill: his feet and stomach were swollen, he was feverish and he was coughing up black and fetid sputum.[3]

Europe's diplomats were quickly buzzing with the news of Edward's sickness. By June officials in Brussels wondered whether he would live. Sir Philip Hoby, ambassador at the court of the Emperor Charles V, reported that in Antwerp those in the know were laying bets on Edward's imminent death and the succession to the throne of his sister Princess Mary. Doubtless reports and gossip were being carried every day by merchants sailing between London and Antwerp. Hoby wrote: 'I pray God our wickedness have not caused God to turn His face aside from us, and to plague us with the most grievous and greatest plague that could come to England, even the taking away of our king, which the Almighty Lord forbid.'[4]

Perhaps even as Hoby was writing his letter, a prayer for the king was said in the chapel of Greenwich Palace. Edward's people asked God to 'look down with thy pitiful eyes upon thy servant Edward our king, and upon this realm of England, professing thy word and holy name'. The life of England's hope and future, the only legitimate heir and successor of King Henry VIII, now lay in God's providence.[5]

In the last months of his life Edward wrote a paper to which he gave the title 'My device for the succession'. He worked at it for a long time, treating it much as he treated his

'Chronicle' – a work in progress he would put away in a drawer of his writing desk, that small and private place where he kept his ink and pens and bric-a-brac. But it was anything but a routine document. The 'Device' set out Edward's intentions for the royal succession after his death, disinheriting his sisters Mary and Elizabeth by leaving the crown of England and Ireland to his cousin Jane Grey.

A whole book could be written solely about the 'Device'. It is so simple and yet so complex a document, a single sheet of folio paper watermarked with eight vertical and parallel lines set twenty-three to twenty-six millimetres apart. At some time in its very long life of 461 years it has been folded horizontally in two places. Close to the upper fold is a small smudge of red sealing wax. On both sides of the sheet is Edward's usual handwriting. He was never a beautiful pen-man, however much he practised with Roger Ascham from Palatino's copybook. In the 'Device' he ran some of his words together, and after dipping the nib of his pen in ink he blotted some of his letters. He altered the document very heavily, making corrections and additions as he wrote and then later striking out sentences and even whole paragraphs.

Probably Edward began the 'Device' in the early spring of 1553 when he was ill but not apparently dying. He had finished it by early June, by which time some thoughts and possibilities set out on paper had become a matter of life-or-death political urgency. At first Edward proposed to leave the crown to a male heir of the family of Lady Frances Grey and her daughters Jane, Katherine and Mary. These four women and girls – Frances was thirty-five years of age, Jane fifteen, Katherine about twelve and Mary about eight – were Edward's blood relatives by Henry VIII's sister Mary and her marriage to Lady Frances's father Charles Brandon, Duke of Suffolk. King Henry had recognized their claim to the English throne in 1544, when in Parliament's third Succession Act 'the heirs of the body of the Lady Frances' came next in the line of royal succession after Edward, Princess Mary and Princess Elizabeth. So what was striking about the 'Device' was not so much Edward's choice of a Grey as his successor, but rather the fact that he leapfrogged the lawful claims of Mary and Elizabeth and challenged quite deliberately the long-dead hand of his father's last will and testament.[6]

The inheritance of a male heir of the Greys was in the spring and early summer of 1553 at best theoretical. But at some point – possibly in May, possibly in June – Edward altered his 'Device' in a hugely significant way. 'To the Lady Jane's heirs male' became 'to the Lady Jane and her heirs male'. In the work of a few seconds, Edward turned a more or less speculative proposal into something of dramatic political immediacy, and a direct challenge to the law of rightful succession. The difficult task is to work out why he did it.[7]

At first we might sniff out a political conspiracy. In May 1553 Lord Guildford Dudley, one of the sons of the Duke of Northumberland, married Lady Jane, a fact which suggests that the king's most powerful adviser leaned on Edward to make Jane his successor. There is not a hint that anyone else other than the king wrote the 'Device' – but was Northumberland looking over Edward's shoulder as he corrected it? Certainly the duke, an ambitious man, had a huge amount to gain from those few movements of the king's pen.

Given the almost complete mystery of the origins of the 'Device' and the circumstances of its composition, we might have here an explanation for it. Equally, we might also be looking at the problem the wrong way round. What if Northumberland, realizing the strength of Edward's belief in the Grey succession through Lady Jane, set up the marriage accordingly? The truth is that we will never know for certain: we can play with the possibilities, aware that any plausible solution leads to further murky questions and uncertainties.

Certainly we can see that Edward was tenacious in believing that the succession was his business as king – that it was for him just as much a prerogative matter as it was to be years later for his sister Elizabeth I. In June 1553, when he expected his advisers to sign up to the 'Device', the judges told him that it was treason for them to do so; he went ahead regardless. For a very sick young man he showed remarkable energy and unshakeable determination.

Edward surely inherited his father's sense of majesty and very likely also his stubbornness. He was after all no ordinary fifteen-year-old. For six years he had listened to preachers comparing him to the kings of the Old Testament who had ruled and reformed God's chosen people. Edward knew that he was God's living representative on earth, and that for his rule he would answer with his soul. And this is one clue to the mystery of the 'Device'. Edward saw and approached the problem of the succession as a king should have done, without sentiment or emotion, conscious always of his duty to God and his people. For Edward there was one question only. Who was best qualified after his death to rule England and Ireland as defender of the faith and

Supreme Head of the Church of England on earth next under God?

Here the 'Device' was the work of Edward's brain and not of his heart. Though on religion Elizabeth's beliefs were straightforwardly acceptable, Princess Mary had always refused to reconcile herself to her brother's Protestant faith and Church settlement. On this the Privy Council and Edward himself pressed her hard in 1551 and 1552. He recorded one encounter between them at Whitehall Palace in March 1551. For too long, Edward's advisers told her, the king had tolerated her Catholic Mass 'in hope of her reconciliation' to the faith established by the law. Mary replied that her soul was God's. The councillors were blunt, saying that (as the king wrote in his 'Chronicle'): 'I constrained not her faith but willed her ... as a subject to obey.' It was obvious that Mary could never govern the Church and so the kingdom of England in the way that Edward and his government would expect her to.[8]

But the greatest impediment to his sisters' succession was their bastardy. Mary was the daughter of Catherine of Aragon; Elizabeth was the daughter of Anne Boleyn. Both, though successors to the crown by act of Parliament and their father's will, were still in law illegitimate. Edward's tests for the royal succession were religion and blood. Where Princess Mary failed both, Princess Elizabeth failed the second only – but it was enough to disqualify her from rule.

So to make sense of the 'Device' we do not have to wrestle with love or a king's feelings of affection for his sisters. As a brother probably he loved them; as a king who ruled in God's name he did not have time for sentiment. Edward's preoccupations were God, duty and kingdom. Power never to be questioned sat easily on his shoulders – he was after all Henry VIII's son and precious jewel.

Ideally Edward wanted a male successor: 'heirs male' is a phrase he wrote twelve times in his 'Device'. The only woman ever to claim the crown of England was Matilda, the daughter of Henry I, in the twelfth century, and that claim was vigorously contested by King Henry's nephew Stephen. Kingship was a man's business and had been so for many centuries. But in June 1553 neither Lady Frances Grey nor Lady Jane was able magically to produce a son out of thin air, so for the time being female succession would have to do. In this novel and peculiar situation it was best to have, not a bastard princess, but the daughter of Henry VIII's niece whose own father, Charles, Duke of Suffolk, had helped to baptize Edward in 1537. Edward made sure that his successor, even though a woman, would have running in her veins Tudor blood untainted by illegitimacy.

Edward's hope in the 'Device' was one day for a king to rule. He considered his own experience: that king might be a boy. In such a minority, his mother would act as his governess, ruling with the advice of at least six councillors out of twenty to be named by Edward in his last will and testament. If the king's mother died before her son reached his eighteenth birthday, England would be governed by Edward's nominated council. When he reached fourteen a future king would be consulted in 'all great matters of importance'. Fourteen was Edward's magic age, and not by accident: this was the age at which he had begun properly to meet his own Privy Council, to work with his secretaries and to write papers on public business – everything that John Cheke's long education in rhetoric and duty had trained him for.

These were the years when Edward's voice was finding its true kingly register. He knew his mind. He gave commands, even to his friends. To Barnaby Fitzpatrick in Paris in December 1551 he wrote with high moral tone:

> For women, as far forth as you may, avoid their company. Yet if the French king command you, you may sometimes dance, so measure be your mean. Else apply yourself to riding, shooting, or tennis, with such honest games. Not forgetting sometime, when you have leisure, your learning, chiefly reading of the Scripture. This I write, not doubting but you would have done so though I had not written, but to spur you on.

In the same letter he gave an unflinchingly factual account of the final disgrace of his uncle the Duke of Somerset, bettered only by the ruthless precision of a single sentence on Somerset's execution in his 'Chronicle': 'The Duke of Somerset had his head cut off upon Tower Hill between eight and nine o'clock in the morning.'[9]

By the age of fourteen the king had grown up. He knew what and who he was, and he was able now to speak for himself. In October 1551 Edward signed a document which, because only a few of his councillors had put their names to it, the Lord Chancellor, Baron Rich, refused to accept. Edward composed a withering letter to Rich that had some force: 'the number of our counsellors or any part of them maketh not our authority.' He was so annoyed by

Rich's assumption that he as king was unable to act for himself that he made a tart entry in his 'Chronicle':

> I wrote a letter that I marvelled that he would refuse to sign that bill or deliver that letter that I had willed any one about me to write. Also that it should be a great impediment for me to send to all my Council and I should seem to be in bondage.

The cat was out of the bag. Edward understood that he was in charge. True, he was not yet eighteen. But his voice mattered. He took advice but he was neither bound nor limited by that advice. It was he who gave commands.[10]

With all of this in mind, we might perhaps imagine Edward reading his 'Device' out loud to himself, intelligent and resolute, knowing his own mind, looking to the future of his people without emotion, compelled by duty: 'For lack of issue of my body. To the Lady Frances's heirs male, if she have any such issue before my death; to the Lady Jane and her heirs male . . .'

In all this perhaps only time was against Edward: time for the Duke of Northumberland to build support, time to isolate Mary and Elizabeth, time to get a new succession law through Parliament, time for Lady Jane Dudley to fall pregnant. But time was too quickly running out.

On Sunday 9 July 1553 eight of the king's privy councillors wrote with instructions to Sir Thomas Cawarden of the Revels Office. It was a dull and routine letter, setting out 'the king's majesty's pleasure' for some tents in Cawarden's custody to be sent to the Tower of London. It seemed hardly worth the time and effort of the one duke, two bishops, one earl, one baron and three knights who signed it at Greenwich Palace.[11]

The really significant thing about the letter is its date. On 9 July 1553 it was impossible for these councillors to know the king's pleasure. Edward had been dead for three days. Even to Cawarden it was a closely guarded secret.

For Edward it was a horrible final illness. On 24 June he could barely breathe. His body was covered in scabs and his nails and hair were falling out. Whatever disease killed him attacked his lungs, taking hold of a young man whose immune system had probably been damaged by smallpox in April 1552. Tuberculosis, bronchopneumonia leading to pleural empyema, a suppurating pulmonary infection leading to generalized septicaemia with renal failure: all of these diagnoses, variously suggested by modern doctors and historians, are plausible from the few observations that survive of the symptoms of Edward's disease.

He died in the privacy of his bedchamber at Greenwich Palace in the company of a few of his most intimate courtiers and servants. With him at the end were Sir Thomas Wroth and Sir Henry Sidney of his Privy Chamber, his physicians Dr Owen and Dr Wendy, and a groom called Christopher Salmon. Edward's last words are supposed to have been 'I am faint; Lord have mercy upon me, and take my spirit.'[12]

His undemonstrative death threw England into a short crisis of succession. Edward's council proclaimed Jane queen, denying with some force the legitimacy of Princess Mary's claim to the throne. They knew from the beginning that the risks were extraordinarily high. Even in putting their names to Edward's 'Device' they had committed treason. Henry VIII's succession law stood. All the legal documents that were drawn up and signed on Edward's orders in June amounted in law to nothing because there had been no time for a parliament to make a new statute of succession. In the short reign of 'Jane the Queen' Edward's former advisers gambled on their success but underestimated Mary's tenacity in claiming the throne. They failed. Not surprisingly, Queen Mary made them pay a heavy price indeed for their treason.

The political chaos of late July and early August 1553 meant that for a whole month Edward's body was unburied. His funeral took place at last in Westminster Abbey on 8 August. He had been brought from Greenwich Palace to the chapel of Whitehall Palace, where his coffin lay upon a structure of wood that was covered in thirty-two yards of black velvet. The chapel was swathed in mourning black from which coats of arms would have stood out in dazzling colours: cloth of gold and silver tissued with gold and silver, 'cloth of gold purple', 'cloth of gold black', blue velvet, white satin, blue and crimson damask, green and white sarsenet.[13]

For a few hours only Edward's court lived again when his old courtiers and officials rode or walked as if they still served the king. Even for those who were free after the collapse of Jane's government it must have felt like a procession of the doomed.

At its centre was the chariot that carried Edward's coffin. On this rested an effigy of the king 'with a crown of gold, and a great collar, and his sceptre in his hand, lying in his robes, and the Garter about his leg, and a coat in embroidery of gold'. From the chariot flew the banners of the Order of the

Garter, a red rose of Lancaster, the arms of Queen Jane Seymour and with deliberate and even provocative incongruity the arms of Queen Mary's mother Catherine of Aragon.[14]

In the procession were the twelve singing children of the Chapel Royal and Will Somers, the king's fool. Present too were the grooms of Edward's Privy Chamber, including Christopher Salmon and John Fowler. Missing was John Cheke. For Cheke, the man who had helped to shape the mind of a king, Mary's reign brought the bitter experiences of arrest, exile, the recantation of his Protestant faith, disgrace and humiliation. Cheke's old teacher in Cambridge, George Day, preached the funeral sermon in Westminster Abbey; he was the bishop who in 1546 had given Prince Edward a New Year's gift of Cicero. Hugh Latimer attended as one of Edward's former chaplains. Later in Mary's reign he was arrested for sedition and burnt at the stake for his Protestant heresy. Thomas Cranmer, Edward's godfather, was like Latimer weeks away from arrest; he was executed in 1556. Present too was Edward's friend and companion and a gentleman of the king's Privy Chamber Barnaby Fitzpatrick.

Edward's coffin was lowered into a small vault only seven and a half feet by two and a half feet, much too narrow for him to be joined later by any other member of his family. He lay then and still lies alone close to the fabulous tomb and chantry chapel of his grandparents Henry VII and Elizabeth of York. At the graveside in the Abbey on 8 August 1553 the old officers of Edward's household broke their staffs and threw them into the vault to mark the end of their service to him.

Notes

PROLOGUE

1. London, British Library, MS Cotton Nero C X, fol. 11ʳ; *The Chronicle and Political Papers of King Edward VI*, ed. by W. K. Jordan (Ithaca, NY: Cornell University Press, 1966), p. 4.
2. Earl of Hertford and Sir Anthony Browne to Sir William Paget, 29 January 1547, London, The National Archives, SP 10/1/1.
3. *Tudor Royal Proclamations*, ed. by P. L. Hughes and J. F. Larkin, 3 vols (New Haven and London: Yale University Press, 1964–9), I, p. 381.

1. 'A PRINCE BORN TO KING HARRY THE EIGHT'

1. London, British Library, MS Cotton Nero C X, fol. 11ʳ; *The Chronicle and Political Papers of King Edward VI*, ed. by W. K. Jordan (Ithaca, NY: Cornell University Press, 1966), p. 3.
2. MS Cotton Nero C X, fol. 2ʳ; Hugh Latimer to Thomas Cromwell, 19 October 1537, *Literary Remains of King Edward the Sixth*, ed. by John Gough Nichols, Roxburghe Club, 2 vols (London: J. B. Nichols and Sons, 1857), I, p. xxiii.
3. *Literary Remains*, I, pp. xxvii–xxx.
4. London, The National Archives, SP 1/133, fol. 240ʳ (*Literary Remains*, I, pp. xxxvii–xxxviii); Lady Bryan to Cromwell, March 1539, SP 1/156, fol. 118ʳ (*Literary Remains*, I, pp. xxxvii–xxxviii).
5. Baron Audley to Cromwell, 8 September 1538, SP 1/136, fol. 86ʳ (*Literary Remains*, I, pp. xxxvi–xxxvii).
6. Simon Thurley, *The Royal Palaces of Tudor England* (New Haven and London: Yale University Press, 1993), pp. 80–81; SP 1/136, fol. 86ʳ.
7. Susan Foister, *Holbein in England* (London: Tate Publishing, 2006), pp. 98–9.
8. *Dynasties: Painting in Tudor and Jacobean England 1530–1630*, ed. by Karen Hearn (London: Tate Publishing, 1995), p. 41; Foister, p. 100; Tracey Sowerby, *Renaissance and Reform in Tudor England: The Careers of Sir Richard Morison c. 1513–1556* (Oxford: Oxford University Press, 2010), p. 137.

2. 'HE WAS BROUGHT UP IN LEARNING'

1. London, British Library, MS Cotton Nero C X, fol. 11ʳ; *The Chronicle and Political Papers of King Edward VI*, ed. by W. K. Jordan (Ithaca, NY: Cornell University Press, 1966), p. 3.
2. Attributed to Sir William Petre, in Roger Ascham, *The Scholemaster* (London: John Day, 1570), sig. B1ᵛ.
3. Roger Ascham, *Toxophilus* (London: Edward Whitchurch, 1545), sig. I2ʳ.
4. London, Lambeth Palace Library, shelf mark [ZZ]1540. 4; *Literary Remains of King Edward the Sixth*, ed. by John Gough Nichols, Roxburghe Club, 2 vols (London: J. B. Nichols and Sons, 1857), I, pp. xxa–xxb.
5. Dr Richard Cox to Sir William Paget, 10 December 1544, SP 1/195, fols 201ʳ–202ʳ; Ascham, *Scholemaster*, sig. B1ᵛ.
6. Prince Edward to Cox, 3 June 1546, *Letters of the Kings of England*, ed. by James Orchard Halliwell, 2 vols (London: Colburn, 1848), II, pp. 10–11; Prince Edward to Cox, 13 September 1546, *Literary Remains*, II, pp. 18–19; monostichs of Dionysius Cato, *Minor Latin Poets*, ed. by J. W. Duff and A. M. Duff (London: William Heinemann, 1934), pp. 585–642.
7. Ascham, *Scholemaster*, sig. B1ᵛ.
8. Prince Edward to Cox, 13 September 1546, *Literary Remains*, II, pp. 18–19; Prince Edward to Cox, 11 March 1546, *Literary Remains*, I, p. 5; *Letters*, II, pp. 5–6.
9. Prince Edward to Henry VIII, 20 June 1546, *Letters*, II, pp. 11–12 (*Literary Remains*, I, pp. 17–18); Prince Edward to Queen Katherine [18 June 1545], MS Cotton Nero C X, fol. 6ʳ; *Katherine Parr: Complete Works and Correspondence*, ed. by Janel Mueller (Chicago: University of Chicago Press, 2011), p. 86.
10. Prince Edward to Queen Katherine, 10 June 1546, *Katherine Parr*, pp. 117–18.
11. Prince Edward to Henry VIII, 4 July 1546, *Letters*, II, p. 14 (*Literary Remains*, I, p. 20).
12. *Katherine Parr*, pp. 119–20.
13. Edward Hall, *The union of the two noble and illustre famelies of Lancastre [and] Yorke*, rev. by Richard Grafton (London: Richard Grafton, 1548), Henry VIII fol. 262ᵛ (sig. xxx4ᵛ).
14. Prince Edward to Henry VIII, 4 September 1546, *Literary Remains*, I, p. 24; Prince Edward to Queen Katherine, 20 September 1546, *Katherine Parr*, p. 121.
15. Prince Edward to Bishop George Day, 25 January 1547, *Literary Remains*, I, pp. 37–8 (*Letters*, II, pp. 24–5); Prince Edward to Archbishop Thomas Cranmer, 24 January 1547, *Literary Remains*, I, p. 36 (*Letters*, II, pp. 23–4).
16. Prince Edward to Princess Mary, 7 November 1546, *Letters*, II, pp. 19–20 (*Literary Remains*, I, pp. 29–30); Prince Edward to Princess Mary, 10 January 1547, *Letters*, II, p. 22 (*Literary Remains*, I, pp. 32–3).
17. *Tudor Royal Proclamations*, ed. by P. L. Hughes and J. F. Larkin, 3 vols (New Haven and London: Yale University Press, 1964–9), I, p. 381.
18. London, The National Archives, PC 2/2, fols 1–9 (31 January 1547), 9–11 (1 February 1547).
19. PC 2/2, fols 48–57 (quotation at fols 48–9).

20. Princess Elizabeth to Edward VI, 14 February 1547, *Elizabeth I: Autograph Compositions and Foreign Language Originals*, ed. by Janel Mueller and Leah S. Marcus (Chicago: University of Chicago Press, 2003), pp. 12–13.

3. 'TO BEAR RULE, AS OTHER KINGS DO'

1. Sir Michael Stanhope to Sir Thomas Cawarden, 5 February 1548, Washington, DC, Folger Shakespeare Library, MS L. b. 290; *Documents relating to the Revels at Court in the time of King Edward VI and Queen Mary*, ed. by Albert Feuillerat (Louvain: A. Uystpruyst, 1914; Nendeln: Kraus Reprint, 1968), p. 33.

2. Thomas Wilson, *The Arte of Rhetorique* (London: Richard Grafton, 1553), sigs b4^v–c1^r; *The Chronicle and Political Papers of King Edward VI*, ed. by W. K. Jordan (Ithaca, NY: Cornell University Press, 1966), pp. 31–2.

3. London, British Library, MS Cotton Nero C X, fol. 11^r (*Chronicle*, p. 3); Roger Ascham, *The Scholemaster* (London: John Day, 1570), fol. 52^r (sig. P4^r).

4. Roger Ascham to Sir William Cecil, 27 September 1552, London, British Library, MS Lansdowne 3, fol. 3^v.

5. *Elizabeth I: Collected Works*, ed. by Leah S. Marcus, Janel Mueller and Mary Beth Rose (Chicago: University of Chicago Press, 2002 edn), pp. 15–16; *Elizabeth I: Autograph Compositions and Foreign Language Originals*, ed. by Janel Mueller and Leah S. Marcus (Chicago: University of Chicago Press, 2003), pp. 14–15.

6. John Fowler's deposition, January 1547, London, The National Archives, SP 10/6/10 (fol. 24^r–^{v}); Edward VI to Queen Katherine, 25 June 1547, *Katherine Parr: Complete Works and Correspondence*, ed. by Janel Mueller (Chicago: University of Chicago Press, 2011), pp. 147–8.

7. SP 10/6/10 (fols 24^v–25^r).

8. John Cheke's deposition, 20 February 1548, SP 10/6/26.

9. Edward VI's deposition, January 1547, *A Collection of State Papers*, ed. by Samuel Haynes (London: William Bowyer, 1740), p. 74 (Hertfordshire, Hatfield House Library, Cecil Papers 150/51); John Fowler to Lord Seymour of Sudeley, 19 July 1548, SP 10/4/31; *Literary Remains of King Edward the Sixth*, ed. by John Gough Nichols, Roxburghe Club, 2 vols (London: J. B. Nichols and Sons, 1857), I, pp. 60–62.

4. 'METHINKS I AM IN PRISON'

1. 9 June 1548, London, The National Archives, SP 10/4/14.

2. London, British Library, MS Cotton Nero C X, fol. 14^r–^{v} (quotation at fol. 14^v); *The Chronicle and Political Papers of King Edward VI*, ed. by W. K. Jordan (Ithaca, NY: Cornell University Press, 1966), pp. 9–10.

3. *Sermons by Hugh Latimer*, ed. by George Elwes Corrie, Parker Society (Cambridge: Cambridge University Press, 1844), pp. 85, 131, 161.

4. 'The Letters of William, Lord Paget of Beaudesert, 1547–1563', ed. by Barrett L. Beer and Sybil M. Jack, *Camden Miscellany XXV*, Camden Society, 4th ser., 13 (1974), pp. 30–32.

5. Sir William Paget to the Duke of Somerset, 8 May 1549, London, The National Archives, SP 10/7/5.

6. MS Cotton Nero C X, fols 14ᵛ-15ʳ (*Chronicle*, pp. 12–13).

7. *A message sent by the kynges Majestie, to certain of his people, assembled in Devon-shire* (London: Richard Grafton, 1549), sig. B5ʳ-ᵛ; *The Remains of Thomas Cranmer, D. D.*, ed. by Henry Jenkyns, 2 vols (Oxford: Oxford University Press, 1833), II, pp. 245–73; John Cheke, *The hurt of sedicion* (London: John Day, 1549), sig. B8ʳ.

8. MS Cotton Nero B X, fol. 16ᵛ (*Chronicle*, p. 17).

9. Edward VI to the Privy Council in London, 8 October 1549, SP 10/9/24.

10. Draft of the Privy Council to Princess Mary and Princess Elizabeth, 9 October 1549, SP 10/9/33.

11. London, The National Archives, PC 2/3, fols 8–10.

12. Archbishop Cranmer, Sir William Paget and Sir Anthony Wingfield to the Privy Council, 11 October 1549, SP 10/9/42.

13. MS Cotton Nero B X, fol. 17ʳ (*Chronicle*, p. 19).

14. MS Cotton Nero B X, fol. 17ʳ (*Chronicle*, p. 19).

15. Robert Graves, *I, Claudius* (Harmondsworth: Penguin Books, 1986), p. 63.

16. *Chronicle*, pp. 36–7.

5. 'A CHALLENGE MADE BY ME'

1. Privy Purse expenses, January 1550–January 1552, London, The National Archives, E 101/426/8; T. A. Birrell, *English Monarchs and their Books: From Henry VII to Charles II* (London: British Library, 1987), pp. 13–14; Werner L. Gundersheimer, *The Life and Works of Louis Le Roy*, Travaux d'Humanisme et Renaissance, 83 (Geneva: Droz, 1966), pp. 11–13.

2. E 101/426/8.

3. W. R. Streitberger, *Court Revels, 1485–1559* (Toronto: University of Toronto Press, 1994), chapter 8.

4. Privy Council warrant to Sir Thomas Cawarden, 8 January 1550, Washington, DC, Folger Shakespeare Library, MS L.b. 275; *Documents relating to the Revels at Court in the time of King Edward VI and Queen Mary*, ed. by Albert Feuillerat (Louvain: A. Uystpruyst, 1914; Nendeln: Kraus Reprint, 1968), pp. 26, 47–9; E 101/426/8; Streitberger, pp. 285–94.

5. *The Report of the Royal Commission of 1552*, ed. by W. C. Richardson (Morgantown: West Virginia University Library, 1974), p. 117; *Revels*, pp. 41, 49; Paul S. Needham, 'John Cheke at Cambridge and court' (unpublished doctoral dissertation, Harvard University, 1971), pp. 201–2, 207.

6. Birrell, p. 13; Pierre Du Ploiche, *A treatise in English and Frenche right necessary and proffitable for al young children* (London: Richard Grafton, 1551), esp. sig. E3ʳ-ᵛ.

7. Robert Recorde, *The pathway to knowledg, containing the first principles of geom-etrie* (London: Reynold Wolfe, 1551); Birrell, pp. 14–15.

8. Andrew Johnston, 'William Paget and the late-Henrician polity' (unpublished doc-toral thesis, University of St Andrews, 2004), p. 39; Simon Thurley, *Whitehall Palace*

(New Haven and London: Yale University Press, 1999), pp. 63–4; *Royal Commission*, p. 126 n. 589; *Literary Remains of King Edward the Sixth*, ed. by John Gough Nichols, Roxburghe Club, 2 vols (London: J. B. Nichols and Sons, 1857), I, pp. xxb–c, describing the horary quadrant, British Museum MLA 1858, 8–21,1; *Humphrey Cole: Mint, Measurement and Maps in Elizabethan England*, ed. by Silke Ackermann, British Museum Occasional Paper, 126 (London: British Museum, 1998), esp. pp. 29–69.

9. E. R. Adair, 'William Thomas', in *Tudor Studies*, ed. by R. W. Seton-Watson (London: Longmans, Green, 1924), pp. 133–60.

10. *The Chronicle and Political Papers of King Edward VI*, ed. by W. K. Jordan (Ithaca, NY: Cornell University Press, 1966), p. 25; London, The British Library, MS Egerton 837 (to Henry, Duke of Suffolk) and MS Royal 17 C X, quotation at fols 1ʳ–2ᵛ (to Edward VI).

11. Felix Raab, *The English Face of Machiavelli* (London and Toronto: Routledge & Kegan Paul, 1964), p. 42.

12. William Thomas, *The historie of Italie* (London: Thomas Berthelet, 1549), fol. 140ʳ (sig. Oo ʳ); Raab, pp. 40–48; MS Cotton B II, fols 2ʳ–31ᵛ; Abraham d'Aubant, *Works of William Thomas* (London: for J. Almon, 1774).

13. MS Cotton Titus B II, fol. 90ʳ.

14. *Chronicle*, p. 57; Streitberger, p. 289.

15. *Chronicle*, pp. 68–9.

16. *Chronicle*, pp. 70–71.

17. *Chronicle*, pp. 72–3.

18. *Chronicle*, pp. 73–5, quotation at p. 73.

19. Sir William Pickering to the Privy Council, 27 October 1551, London, The National Archives, SP 68/9/95.

6. 'MY DEVICE FOR THE SUCCESSION'

1. *Documents Relating to the Revels at Court in the time of King Edward VI and Queen Mary*, ed. by Albert Feuillerat (Louvain: A. Uystpruyst, 1914; Nendeln: Kraus Reprint, 1968), p. 145; W. R. Streitberger, *Court Revels, 1485–1559* (Toronto: University of Toronto Press, 1994), p. 293.

2. *Literary Remains of King Edward the Sixth*, ed. by John Gough Nichols, Roxburghe Club, 2 vols (London: J. B. Nichols and Sons, 1857), I, p. clxxxv.

3. Sir William Petre to Sir William Cecil, 7 May 1553, *A Collection of State Papers*, ed. by Samuel Haynes (London: William Bowyer, 1740), p. 149 (Hertfordshire, Hatfield House, Cecil Papers 151/103).

4. Sir Philip Hoby to Sir William Cecil, 25 June 1553, *State Papers*, p. 154 (Cecil Papers 198/49–50).

5. *A Prayer sayd in the kinges Chappell in the tyme of hys graces Sicknes* (London: William Copland, 1553).

6. *Statutes of the Realm*, ed. by A. Luders and others, 11 vols (London: George Eyre and Andrew Strahan, 1810–28), III, pp. 955–8.

7. London, The Inner Temple, Petyt MS 538/47, fol. 317.

8. *The Chronicle and Political Papers of King Edward VI*, ed. by W. K. Jordan (Ithaca, NY: Cornell University Press, 1966), p. 55.
9. Edward VI to Barnaby Fitzpatrick, 20 December 1551, *Literary Remains*, I, pp. 70–71; *Chronicle*, p. 107.
10. Draft of Edward VI to Richard, Baron Rich, 1 October 1551, London, The National Archives, SP 10/13/55; London, British Library, MS Cotton Nero C X, fol. 43ʳ (*Chronicle*, p. 84).
11. Washington, DC, Folger Shakespeare Library, MS L. b. 503.
12. *Literary Remains*, I, p. cxcix.
13. 'The Accompte of Sir Edwarde Waldegrave' ed. by Craven Ord, *Archaeologia*, 12 (January 1794), pp. 334–96 (quotation at p. 335).
14. *Literary Remains*, I, p. ccxl.

Further Reading

Romantic, at times breathless, but always lively is Hester W. Chapman, *The Last Tudor King: A Study of Edward VI* (London: Jonathan Cape, 1961). There are two useful companion volumes by W. K. Jordan. The first, *Edward VI: The Young King* (London: George Allen & Unwin, 1968), covers the years of the Duke of Somerset's protectorate. The second, *Edward VI: The Threshold of Power* (London: George Allen & Unwin, 1970), considers the political ascendancy of the Duke of Northumberland. Though often impenetrably dense, David Loades's *John Dudley Duke of Northumberland, 1504–1553* (Oxford: Clarendon Press, 1996) is the best account we have of Northumberland's government. Jennifer Loach, *Edward VI*, edited by George Bernard and Penry Williams (New Haven and London: Yale University Press, 1999) is the standard academic study of Edward's life and reign. Diarmaid MacCulloch, *Tudor Church Militant: Edward VI and the Protestant Reformation* (London: Allen Lane, 1999) is a penetrating analysis of Edward's Church and the scouring Reformation of his reign, on which see also Professor MacCulloch's *Thomas Cranmer* (New Haven and London: Yale University Press, 1996). The best modern narrative history of Edward's reign is Chris Skidmore, *Edward VI: The Lost King of England* (London: Weidenfeld & Nicolson, 2007). For a careful and persuasive account of Edward's 'Device' and its significance see E. W. Ives, *Lady Jane Grey: A Tudor Mystery* (Chichester: Wiley-Blackwell, 2009). The outstanding study of Edward and his sisters Princess Mary and Princess Elizabeth is John Guy, *The Children of Henry VIII* (Oxford: Oxford University Press, 2013).

Still the best collection of documents on Edward's life and reign, in two volumes, is John Gough Nichols, *Literary Remains of King Edward the Sixth* (London: J. B. Nichols and Sons, 1857). Important and far more accessible than Nichols (though for specialists not without its problems) is *The Chronicle and Political Papers of King Edward VI*, edited by W. K. Jordan (Ithaca, NY: Cornell University Press, 1966). The first biography of Edward, by Sir John Hayward, was published in 1630. Like any work of history from the seventeenth century it has to be used with great care and is best approached in Barrett L. Beer, *The life and raigne of King Edward the Sixth* (Kent, OH and London: Kent State University Press, 1993). At first overwhelming in its detail but excellent for the information it provides on the departments and personnel of Edward's court and household is *The Report of the Royal Commission of 1552*, edited by W. C. Richardson (Morgantown, VA: West Virginia University Library, 1974).

Picture Credits

1. Edward VI as a child, *c.*1538, by Hans Holbein the Younger (National Gallery of Art, Washington, DC/Bridgeman Images)
2. Thomas Seymour, second half of the 16th century, English School (National Portrait Gallery, London/Bridgeman Images)
3. Jane Seymour, 1536, by Hans Holbein the Younger (Kunsthistorisches Museum, Vienna/Bridgeman Images)
4. Edward VI, *c.*1546, by William Scrots (attr.) (The Royal Collection Trust © Her Majesty Queen Elizabeth II, 2014/ Bridgeman Images)
5. Edward VI coronation medal, 1547 (© The Trustees of the British Museum. All Rights Reserved. [CM EngM.1/PI 755])
6. John Cheke, mid-16th century, by Claude Corneille de Lyon (attr.) (Courtesy of Barnsley Metropolitan Borough Council Arts, Museums and Archives Service, Cannon Hall Museum Collection)
7. King Edward VI, *c.*1550, by William Scrots (attr.) (Compton Verney, Warwickshire. Photo: © Compton Verney.)
8. King Edward VI, *c.*1551, by William Scrots (attr.) (© RMN-Grand Palais [Musée du Louvre]/Thierry Ollivier)
9. *King Edward VI and the Pope, c.*1570, English School (National Portrait Gallery, London/Bridgeman Images)
10. 'The Lord Protectors arguing in front of the boy king at a Council of State', illustration by Frank Hampson from *Kings and Queens: Book Two* by L. Du Garde Peach (© Ladybird Books Ltd, 1968. Illustration used under licence from Ladybird Books Ltd.)

Acknowledgements

Simon Winder commissioned and edited this book with his customary energy and enthusiasm, and I owe to him and to Peter Robinson the wonderful opportunity to have been able to write it. The team at Penguin, especially Marina Kemp and Pen Vogler, are always fantastically supportive, even once offering tea and shelter to a waif-and-stray author stranded in London by a freak storm. I am most grateful to Linden Lawson and Anna Hervé for their skilful copy-editing of the text.

To John Guy, John Cramsie, Alan Bryson and Guy Perry I owe debts of gratitude for many favours, kindnesses and impositions. I must thank Michael Frost of the Inner Temple Library and many other librarians and archivists who have helped me. I am very grateful to Jane Rickard and Martin Butler for inviting me to talk about Edward VI to the School of English at Leeds, and to Lena Oetzel, Kerstin Weiand and Scott C. Lucas for giving me the opportunity to join a panel at the Sixteenth Century Studies Conference in Puerto Rico. The intellectual energy of Leeds and the sunshine of San Juan helped me in all sorts of ways to finish this book.

I should like to thank for their support Paul Cooke of the Faculty of Arts and Michael Brennan of the Leeds Humanities Research Institute; the Leeds International Conference Fund for a very generous travel grant; the research fund of the School of History; and the generosity of Graham Loud, Malcolm Chase and Will Gould. All of my colleagues and students in the School of History have been unfailingly supportive, lively and generous, and I thank them very warmly indeed.

Max is the best and most perceptive critic of my work. Even the most effusive Tudor rhetoric could never thank her enough for everything she is and does. This short book is dedicated to our wonderful Matilda, a very small gift offered to her by an extraordinarily fortunate father.

Stephen Alford
Gargrave
April 2014

Index